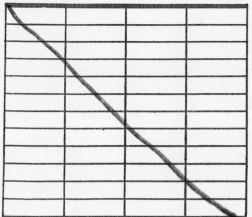

IT'S YOUR MOVE

Expressive Movement Activities
for the Language Arts Class

IT'S YOUR MOVE

Expressive Movement Activities for the Language Arts Class

GLORIA T. BLATT

Oakland University
Rochester, Michigan

JEAN CUNNINGHAM

University of British Columbia
Vancouver, B.C.
Canada

Teachers College, Columbia University
New York & London, 1981

Published by Teachers College Press
1234 Amsterdam Avenue
New York, N.Y. 10027

Library of Congress Cataloging in Publication Data

Blatt, Gloria T., 1924-
  It's your move.

  Includes bibliographies and index.
  1. Language arts (Elementary) 2. Movement
education. I. Cunningham, Jean. II. Title.
LB1576.B498   372.6   81-9014

ISBN 0-8077-2687-7   AACR2
ISBN 0-8077-2640-0 (pbk.)

Manufactured in the United States of America

86 85 84 83 82 81   1 2 3 4 5 6

Copyright information is continued on page ix.

Contents

I. DESIGNING
MOVEMENT/LANGUAGE-ARTS LESSONS

II. MODEL LESSONS

Preface

During the hopeful days just after the Second World War, the British educational system underwent a profound change that was felt at all school levels and particularly in the infant schools, for the youngest children. For the first time, leaders tried to meet the educational needs of all children from all walks of life by planning curricula that would ensure school success. They were guided by Susan Isaacs' trend-setting research, which paralleled Piaget's work and indicated, among other things, that children learn best from concrete experience.

One of the most significant changes in the entire curriculum took place in physical education. Rudolph Laban, an efficiency expert and dancer, had noticed that young children used a very narrow range of body movements and that they could learn to expand range and quality through direct instruction. He devised a new curriculum and named it "educational movement." Direct teaching was used to help the children try out different body movements, gradually expanding what they were able to do.

Teachers welcomed the new curriculum because there was little emphasis on competition, because the children enjoyed it, and because many of the teachers quickly realized that movement was a vehicle for self-expression and for learning a variety of school subjects—mathematics, music, science, and language arts. Today, movement has a firm place in the British educational system at all levels from infant to secondary schools.

Although increasingly used in countries other than England, movement has been relatively slow to emerge in the American school curriculum. This book is designed for teachers who are inexperienced in movement education and who want to take advantage of it as an aid in teaching and learning.

The ideas and lessons explained in this book grow directly out of the English infant school experience. As in British schools, movement is used here to help children expand the range and quality of their body motions, express their own feelings and ideas, and create their own dances. Particular stress is placed on integrating movement with language and literature so that the latter are more meaningful and exciting. Teachers who try the ideas explained in this book will find expressive movement a powerful tool for enhancing learning both in physical education and in language arts.

REPRINT ACKNOWLEDGMENTS

This section is a continuation of the copyright page.

"Bundles" (excerpt). Reprinted by permission of the Yale University Press from *Songs for Parents*, by John Farrar, 1921.

"Fireworks." From *The Blackbird in the Lilac* by James Reeves (1952). Reprinted by permission of Oxford University Press.

"Get Up, Blues." From *A Chisel in the Dark* by James A. Emanuel (Detroit: Lotus Press, 1980). Also appears in *Black Out Loud: An Anthology of Modern Poems by Black Americans*, ed. Arnold Adoff (New York: Macmillan, 1970). Reprinted by permission of James A. Emanuel.

"Hist Whist." Reprinted from *Tulips & Chimneys* by E. E. Cummings, with the permission of Liveright Publishing Corporation. Copyright 1923, 1925 and renewed 1951, 1953 by E. E. Cummings. Copyright © 1973, 1976 by Nancy T. Andrews. Copyright © 1973, 1976 by George James Firmage.

"A Lazy Thought." From *There Is No Rhyme for Silver* by Eve Merriam. Copyright © 1962 by Eve Merriam. Reprinted by permission of the author.

"The Main-Deep." Reprinted with permission of Macmillan Publishing Co., Inc. and Macmillan Press, Ltd. from *Collected Poems* by James Stephens. Copyright 1925, 1926 by Macmillan Publishing Co., Inc., renewed 1953, 1954 by James Stephens.

"Ping-Pong." From *Finding a Poem* by Eve Merriam. Copyright © 1970 by Eve Merriam. Reprinted by permission of the author.

"Roads." Reprinted with permission of Macmillan Publishing Co., Inc. from *Poems* by Rachel Field. Copyright 1924, 1930 by Macmillan Publishing Co., Inc.

"Roadways." Reprinted with permission of Macmillan Publishing Co., Inc. and The Society of Authors (London) from *Poems* by John Masefield. Copyright 1912 by Macmillan Publishing Co., Inc., renewed 1940 by John Masefield.

"Seesaw," by Evelyn Beyer. From *Another Here and Now Story Book*, by Lucy Sprague Mitchell. Copyright 1937 by E. P. Dutton & Co., Inc., renewal, 1965, by Lucy Sprague Mitchell. Reprinted by permission of the publisher, E. P. Dutton.

"Shadows." From Patricia Hubbell, *Catch Me a Wind* (New York: Atheneum, 1968). Copyright © 1968 by Patricia Hubbell. Used with the permission of Atheneum Publishers.

"Song of the Train." From *Far and Few* by David McCord. Copyright ©

1952 by David McCord. Reprinted by permission of Little, Brown and Company.

"Stop—Go." From *I Like Automobiles* by Dorothy Baruch (New York: John Day, 1931). Reprinted by permission of the author.

"The Term." From *Collected Earlier Poems* of William Carlos Williams. Copyright 1938 by New Directions Publishing Corporation. Reprinted by permission of New Directions.

"Visit." From *Miracles: Poems by Children of the English-Speaking World*, ed. Richard Lewis. Copyright © 1966 by Richard Lewis. Reprinted by permission of Simon & Schuster, a Division of Gulf & Western Corporation.

"Wild Iron." From *An Anthology of New Zealand Verse*, comp. Robert Chapman & Jonathan Bennett (New York: Oxford University Press, 1956). Reprinted by permission of the author, Allen Curnow.

"The Wind Has Wings." From *The Wind Has Wings*, comp. by Mary Alice Downie & Barbara Robertson (New York: Walck, 1968). Reprinted by permission of Oxford University Press.

IT'S YOUR MOVE

Expressive Movement Activities
for the Language Arts Class

1

Introduction

For many years experts in literature for children have strongly maintained that after a poem or story is read in class, children need to express how they feel, as well as what they understand. Most have agreed that children can best respond to literature through the arts—by drawing pictures, doing dramatizations, writing, or dancing. In recent years leaders in language arts have also argued that youngsters can use the same art forms to express their own ideas and feelings while they expand language. Although few teachers question such arguments, not many feel comfortable when they deal with the arts in the classroom, particularly when the focus is on movement, which is a relatively new school subject in the United States.

THE PURPOSE OF THIS BOOK

We have prepared this book to provide educators with guides for developing and using movement in the context of the language arts and literature curricula in the elementary school classroom. Included are complete model lessons integrating expressive movement, language arts, and literature; an explanation of the theory behind movement; explicit directions for planning lessons; and lists of many resources. After reading and using the material in this book, elementary and middle school teachers will know numerous ways to enrich lessons in literature, language arts, and reading with expressive movement.

EXPRESSIVE MOVEMENT—A DEFINITION

In her book *Movement Education*,[1] Marion North points out that there are two kinds of human movement. The first, body language, expresses the individual's inner state of mind revealed in postures, hand gestures, and the like. The second, functional movement used in the ordinary pursuits of living, includes activities like running, walking, and jumping.

When teachers of physical education use the term "movement education," they draw a distinction between the functional movements that characterize gymnastics and the expressive movements of dance. Since dance is expressive only when it conveys ideas and feelings, there is some dance which is functional. Square dance, for example, is primarily concerned with floor patterns and traditional steps. The term "expressive movement" refers to the guided exploration of children's movement ideas and improvisations and the creation of improvised dances.

EXPRESSIVE MOVEMENT— A CREATIVE ACTIVITY

We agree with Jerome Bruner, who defines creativity as "effective surprise."[2] Carl Rogers, who characterizes creativity in the same way as Bruner, describes the creative process as "playing spontaneously with ideas, colors, shapes, relationships, to juggle elements into impossible juxtapositions."[3] Conditions for creativity are set, according to him, when (1) the individual is accepted as worthy without condition, and (2) a climate of external evaluation is absent.

In expressive movement, children work at three levels. They first become acquainted with movement elements, trying different ways of walking, running, jumping, sliding, balancing, and rolling. Differences may involve speed, body shape, or closeness to the floor.

---

[1]Marion North, *Movement Education* (New York: Dutton, 1973).

[2]Jerome Bruner, *On Knowing: Essays for the Left Hand* (Cambridge, Mass.: Harvard University, Belknap Press, 1962).

[3]Carl Rogers, *Creativity*, ed. P. E. Vernon (Hammondswork, Middlesex, England: Penguin Books, 1970).

Later they learn to link two or three of these movements together to form a pattern or sequence of actions deliberately designed to include some different or contrasting movement elements. Finally, they may work with techniques they already know to polish individual selections.

At the first level, the children are becoming acquainted with the elements of movement. They take a first step toward creativity when the teacher encourages them to solve movement problems in divergent ways by setting tasks like: "Find three different ways to curl up very small."

Although considerable direct teaching occurs at this level, the children learn that their own solutions to movement problems need not be the same as those of others. They also learn that their efforts will be accepted by the teacher because no external evaluations take place.

The children take a second step toward creativity when they experiment with sequences of movement that highlight complementary or contrasting actions. Now they begin to play with relationships, juggling elements in interesting and sometimes "impossible juxtapositions."

Transition from the first to the second level may occur in two ways. Often children spontaneously improvise patterns or sequences of movement as they explore basic movements. At other times, their teachers may lead them into preplanned sequences. In either case, true creativity occurs when children synthesize their knowledge of movement in unique responses to stimuli of various sorts. Whether teacher or children take the initiative, children can eventually invent their own dances, just as they write their own stories, paint their own pictures, or create their own dramatic scenes.

To highlight the creative nature of movement, the first level, which is often called movement training in books dealing with movement education, is called *exploration* in this book. The second level is called *improvisation* to underline the spontaneous, tentative nature of dance at this stage. To stress the point that work may also be carefully planned and skills sharpened from time to time, the third level is called *dance composition*. This book does not deal directly with dance composition because the emphasis is on dance as an improvised response to literature and language.

EXPRESSIVE MOVEMENT AND
PHYSICAL DEVELOPMENT

Movement is important for its own sake. Children exposed to it are helped to become both physically fit and skillful in a variety of situations as they increase their coordination and abilities. Their competence is developed in a natural way through self-discipline and self-reliance. Working out their own ideas in pairs and groups, their social awareness is enhanced, and their motor skills advance according to individual ability, readiness, and interest. Last but not least, expressive movement introduces children to the rudiments of an art form, giving them the tools for using dance in its basic form.

Perhaps expressive movement is successful as a physical activity because competition is avoided. All the children share all the roles at the same time. Each child participates, adding something individual to a creative interpretation. In a class improvising a story about a witch, everyone is the witch. All the children have the experience of feeling witch-like; all learn from and contribute to the imaginative insights of others.

EXPRESSIVE MOVEMENT AND
THE LANGUAGE ARTS

Every language arts program in the elementary school has one overriding objective: to foster meaningful communication through which children can build and refine their language abilities. Most normal children come to school conversant with the oral language spoken at home. It becomes the job of the school to help boys and girls expand that knowledge into other areas of language, such as reading and writing.

One of the best ways to help children communicate is to create a setting in which language is used without barriers drawn between reading, writing, speaking, and listening. Rather than directly teaching children the "skill" of listening, for instance, situations are arranged in which boys and girls listen and then interact by speaking, reading, and writing. Such an approach is effective because it builds on the fact that communication is a fluid, many-faceted process demanding interaction among all its elements.

Movement is especially valuable in promoting this process. Movement lessons enhance integration of the language arts by providing effective bridges among all elements of communication. For example, children can listen to and read literary selections, later responding through movement to the meaning, rhythm, or mood. After improvising a movement composition, talk, reading, and writing grow quite naturally out of the experience.

Movement also heightens expression by creating situations in which children must listen carefully, use oral language precisely, and think in depth about what they have read. Even creative writing is affected very directly.

The next paragraphs discuss some ways in which movement enhances the language arts.

Listening

In most classes children listen passively. Intermittently, they play a kind of verbal ping pong with the teacher, who serves up a question while selected children return the ball in the form of an answer. The rest of the children, who have no direct need to answer, may well ignore the teacher altogether, many not listening unless they think they will be called on.

Movement lessons help children listen carefully. Youngsters are more attentive if lessons provide conditions where they have something to listen for, if they are given specific training, and if all of them must respond. Many movement lessons demand immediate responses to directions by everyone in the group; some call for children to discriminate between various stimuli; others ask children to listen critically so that they can create a sequence that captures some aspect of a selection—a mood, rhythm, or theme. A simple game like "Traffic" (exploration 2, chapter 5) requires that young listeners respond quickly to direction. During "A Lazy Thought" (lesson 6, chapter 6), on the other hand, the teacher asks the children to listen and discriminate between moods and rhythm.

Speaking

Movement lessons frequently set the scene for many varieties of oral language in the classroom, for example, occasions when literature can be read aloud in chorus or individually. Many movement lessons also lend themselves to follow-up work in creative drama and other forms of oral composition. Children first explore how people move or stand (as in exploration 23, chapter 5) and later dramatize a story around the action involved in the exploration. Groups of children could then discuss what they did and why. Frequently, movement lessons are vivid enough to spark children's imaginations and memories. After "Roads" (lesson 1, chapter 7), for instance, children are often interested in sharing their own traveling experiences.

Reading

Oral reading frequently improves after groups of children interpret poems or stories in chorus. Because the group may go over the same selection several times, even the slowest readers learn to read the selections more accurately and with expression.

Movement can also be a vehicle for improving reading comprehension. Vocabulary ranging anywhere from function words (i.e., "with," "under," "over") to difficult abstract vocabulary may be learned through dance. The children become acquainted with the words through work at the blackboard; later they take cues for movement from printed words. The movement itself teaches them the meanings of the words. As a result, reading comprehension is deepened.

Through movement, the children not only broaden their vocabularies, but are able to grasp the concrete meaning of a selection by exploring its mood, rhythm, and figurative language. In "The Term" (lesson 3, chapter 7), for example, the children use their own bodies to compare a human body and a sheet of brown paper run over by a car. They quickly understand that the poem suggests that human beings have a limited life span, whereas lifeless objects may survive and seem untouched by some accidents of time.

Creative Writing

According to Margaret Langdon,[4] children do their best writing when they feel something intensely, when they describe their own ideas and thoughts, and when their writing grows out of direct sen-

---

[4]Margaret Langdon, *Let the Children Write* (London: Longman, 1961).

sory experience. They are most successful if they have some kind of structure around which they can create an idea or story, for instance, a story starter, the framework of a story they are familiar with, or an experience that they or someone they know has had.

Unfortunately, teachers frequently have trouble generating good classroom compositions because children are asked to write about topics that are not vital to their communication needs. Also, assignments frequently fail to grow from direct sensory experience or to allow time for playing with ideas. Young people tend to write what they think will please a teacher, rather than what they really have on their minds.

Expressive movement overcomes these difficulties. During movement lessons children often are carried away by the action emotionally, and their excitement bubbles over into the writing lesson that follows. The movement lessons themselves are direct sensory experiences linked to specific words from which dance sequences are built. There is ample time to play with ideas; the writing process is not short-circuited. Indeed, movement lessons are structured so that creativity is enhanced. The results are frequently exciting, effective writing.

Typical of the interaction between movement and language is the work of children in a fifth-sixth grade group who had listened to an Eskimo chant, "The Wind Has Wings," in which the wind is likened to evil spirits hovering over their prey. (This poem and a movement lesson based on it are given in chapter 2.) After the movement activities (which included exploring the meanings of action words like *claw*, *twist*, and *tear*) the children wrote the following wind poems:

> The wind is like an angry, evil, spirit,
> Leaping and tossing.
> Touching you with cold, clammy fingers.
> It is chasing along the dark road,
> Hovering over the forest,
> Tearing and twisting with enormous strength,
> Ripping and pushing the dark heavy clouds.
> It haunts in the quiet city and
> Is scared when the sun comes up.
> —Ralph, 5th Grade

The sighing wind is soft.
Like a little baby's skin,
It moans around on a sunny day,
and rustles the trees,
With its sighing breeze,
The sighing wind.
—Carl, 5th Grade

The wind bites with its long sharp teeth
It steals umbrella tops, rips wires from their poles,
Plays on tree tops, rustles the dead, dead leaves.
When the winds of North, South, West, and East join
Hands, they become the lashing hurricane.
It brings winter to the land,
That's the bitter bite of the wind.
—Jan, 6th Grade

Literature

In the turbulent world of twentieth-century North America, facts and figures bombard us constantly with more information than we can assimilate. Newspapers, magazines, books, almanacs, and television report on the tragedies and comedies of living with endless detail and without organization. In contrast, literature takes the stuff of life and organizes it meaningfully. At the same time that we learn about the human condition, we learn how and often why it happened. We see the world reflected and organized in the mirror provided by literature.

Literature can also take us beyond the real into an imaginary world, delighting us with stories and poems about people and places that we have never encountered or that never existed. Whether entry be through the looking glass of Alice or the poetry of Shel Silverstein, literature can give readers experiences that fire their imaginations and delight them with a special magic.

Regardless of subject, technique, or author's purpose, because written language is the medium of communication, the literary experience is vicarious. Creative drama changes vicarious literary experiences into living ones. As children translate a story into action, the story line, the people, the setting, as well as the ideas become real. Children acting out Toad's escape from prison in *The Wind in the Willows* enjoy working directly through the story, experiencing the situation in depth, finding out the kinds of personalities Toad and the others in the story really have, relating words to action, exploring the feelings of the people in the story, and learning to relate emotionally.

Like drama, movement also changes vicarious literary experience into vivid living involvement. Character or story line can be developed into a dance-drama, as well as into a creative drama. An example of dance-drama, "Orion," may be found in chapter 7 (lesson 8). Using an approach that grows out of movement exploration, the children examine the way the small but deadly Scorpion kills the mighty Orion, the actions of Scorpion, the heaving and suffering of the dying Orion, the dramatic intergalactic atmosphere.

While creative drama and expressive movement are both useful in dramatizing stories, poetry without a story line is best interpreted through expressive movement. Movement gives poetry a concrete reality, immediacy, and excitement while children explore the poem for dominant ideas, themes, mood, imagery, or rhythm. In the interpretation of "Hist Whist," by E. E. Cummings (lesson 4, chapter 7), for instance, the youngsters experience the rhythm, play with the sounds, and explore the movements of "ghost things" twitching.

Most educators agree that at the elementary school level first priority in the literature program should be enjoyment rather than literary criticism. Most also agree that children enjoy literature more if they are aware of literary elements. When movement is used as a response to literature, both objectives are met. Movement interpretations that focus on literary components provide readers with an in-depth literary experience, one in which they can explore the structure of literature without resorting to analysis.

Language Development

Educational and psychological research suggest other reasons why movement is an important asset in the classroom. Piaget, Bruner, and others have shown that children first understand the meaning of objects through movement and sensory experience.[5] A baby

---

[5]For information on learning meaning as an aspect of language development, turn to: Jerome Bruner & J. J. Goodnow, *A Study of Thinking* (New York: Wiley, 1956); Jean Piaget, *Language and Thought of the Child* (London: Routledge and Kegan

responds to a ball by handling it; by feeling its texture, weight, and size; by seeing it roll and bounce; perhaps by putting it in his or her mouth. When an older person calls it a "ball," the infant learns to associate word and sensory experience.

This mode of learning meaning is commonly used by young children, as shown in the definitions given by preschoolers in Ruth Krauss's well-known book *A Hole Is to Dig:*[6]

Mashed potatoes are to give everyone enough.

A face is to help you make faces.

Dogs are to kiss people.

By the time they are eight or nine and beginning to think in abstract terms, children place objects and ideas with which they have had experience in categories. But when they are unfamiliar with a concept, they revert to sensory definitions. They can state that potatoes, beans, or peas are vegetables, but like the children quoted below, they may define "freedom," which represents a more difficult concept, through sensory experience:

Freedom is when nobody can stop you.—8-year-old

Freedom is when you can go someplace without anyone.—10-year-old

Freedom is when you can do anything you want.—7-year-old

When movement and oral interpretation are associated, children are constantly forced to relate sensory experience and words. Movement paralleling natural patterns of language learning helps make a story or poem more meaningful.

Piaget suggests another important reason why movement should be part of teaching. He notes that children must play an active part in their own learning and maintains, "Knowledge is derived from ac-

---

Paul, 1968); L. S. Vygotsky, *Thought and Language* (Cambridge, Mass.: M.I.T. Press, 1962); and A. F. Watts, *The Language and Mental Development of Children* (London: George C. Harrap, 1966).

[6]Ruth Krauss, *A Hole Is to Dig* (New York: Harper & Row, 1952).

tion. To learn an object is to act on it and transform it."[7] Children interpreting literary selections through expressive movement are, in fact, transforming selections from a verbal form to preverbal experiences.

Expressing Emotions

Common sense suggests still other reasons why movement fits so comfortably into the language arts program. Young children who are angry or frustrated often express their feelings by throwing tantrums; youngsters who are happy are likely to jump for joy. Teachers who have just received a pay raise may well go off whistling, a new bounce in their step. All of us express our feelings in our movements throughout our lives. Creative movement simply offers a channeled outlet for expressing emotions in a natural fashion. Making a monster with their own bodies (as in lesson 8, chapter 6) may help youngsters deal with their fears. Simulating the motion of the ocean ("Wild Iron," lesson 5, chapter 7) will help children feel the excitement and wonder of the sea. Once they are familiar with and feel free to use creative movement, children will often use their newly developed abilities to express personal and emotional needs. Writing as well as discussion, appreciation, and comprehension of literature are deeply affected.

USING THIS BOOK

Directions for planning lessons are presented in chapters 2, 3, and 4. These chapters will give teachers an initial sense of how movement lessons are planned. They include complete guides for classroom management, basic principles of teaching movement, useful hints on light and sound effects, and general methods for integrating movement and language arts.

A series of complete demonstration lessons combining movement and language arts will be found in chapters 5, 6, and 7. Each lesson models a way to develop an exploration or improvisation. After first reading the chapters on planning, teachers should try the

---

[7]Jean Piaget, *The Science of Education and the Psychology of the Child* (New York: Orion, 1970).

model lessons in their classes, gradually becoming familiar with movement principles through repeated practice and then use the same or other selections listed in the bibliographies to develop original improvisations or explorations. The lessons are intended to help teachers work toward a time when they and their children will feel comfortable enough to explore and improvise on their own.

The lessons in this book have been developed around literature and the language arts. They spell out ways to involve children in active responses to language, stories, and poems that at the same time enhance communication. The lessons also set the scene for further experiences in drama, discussion, reading, and writing and, therefore, provide a unifying element for an integrated language arts program. Suggestions for extending the movement lessons to other language arts are included with each lesson in chapters 6 and 7.

When teachers have worked through the entire book, it is wise to return to chapter 2 and reread principles of movement analysis, which are the key to designing exciting, effective improvisations. Once teachers have completed work in Sections I and II, they are ready to embark on a complete classroom program that uses expressive movement effectively.

SUMMARY

It's Your Move is intended as a guide for teachers using movement in the language arts class. It lays out an agenda in which children first learn how to move in a variety of ways and later improvise dances around exploratory movements.

The lessons found in this book are valuable as teaching tools in a number of ways. Boys and girls develop new physical powers while learning to listen carefully, to use oral language effectively, and to read and write better. Most important, lessons like those described here allow children to respond intellectually and emotionally to stories and poems they read.

I

DESIGNING
MOVEMENT/
LANGUAGE-ARTS
LESSONS

2

Planning The Movement Lesson

To use movement effectively, teachers should know something about movement or dance as an art without reference to the language arts. After they learn to observe movement with a critical eye, teachers will be able to design movement lessons that use a variety of stimuli, including language, literature, and music.

An important first step in learning about movement is to understand how to describe body action with a consistent vocabulary. Any well-thought-out, easily understood system is satisfactory. In this book a simplified classification from Rudolph Laban's movement analysis is used.[1] Children learn the terminology very quickly as they relate the concepts to sensory experience. It is also important to develop techniques for guiding children during movement lessons. This chapter discusses these basic elements. With the information presented here, the teacher will be able to design the movement segment of the movement/language-arts lessons.

DESCRIBING MOVEMENT

Movement can be described in general terms by stating:

What action the body is performing.
Where in the surrounding space it is taking place.
How or with what speed, strength, and "flow."
Relationship with partner or group.

---

[1]*Modern Educational Dance* (1963).

Each of the four categories—*what*, *where*, *how*, and *relationship*—has a number of subdivisions, which are listed in Table 1. With these four categories we can describe any movement completely. The fourth is particularly important in educational movement.

Suppose we describe the movement of a fish in a tank using the four categories. We may tell *what* the fish does by stating the traveling actions he performs, in this case, darting and gliding. The tank is the space in which the fish swims. We may describe *where* he

Table 1. Movement Analysis

What[1]	Where[2]	How	Relationship
Body Actions	**Direction**	**Time**	**Individual**
Traveling	Forward	Varies from quick and	
Jumping	Backward	sudden to slow and	
Stretching	Sideways	sustained.	
Curling			
Twisting			
Turning			
Rising			
Falling			
Body Shape	**Level**	**Force**	**Partner or Group Work**
Stretching Wide	High	Varies from firm,	MATCHING ACTION
Stretching Thin	Medium	strong to light,	Mirroring
Twisted	Low	fine action.	Following/Leading
Curled			
		Flow	WORK IN UNISON
		Varies from free,	Together/Synchronized
		fluent movement to	Working in Succession
		stopped or held	Working at Different
		movement (bound	Times
		flow).	
			ACTION/REACTION
			Child responds to partner's
			actions

[1]Whole body or parts of the body (arms, legs, etc.) may be used for actions or shapes.

[2]When direction and level are combined they may be used to form pathways, which are traced on the floor or in the air. Pathways may be straight, angular, curved, or twisted.

swims by stating that he changes direction continually, sometimes diving to the floor of the tank, then swimming up toward the surface around and through the plants. At times he moves swiftly or suddenly, now and then slowly. On occasion, the flow of this movement is arrested altogether as he remains motionless, thus changing *how* he moves. Describing a *relationship* with another fish, the two sometimes swim next to each other; on other occasions one or the other leads.

Actions often emphasize different aspects of movement, but to describe an individual movement, we must use all four categories: *what* body actions are being performed; *where* they occur in space; *how* or with what speed, force and flow they are performed; and the *relationship* of individuals performing the actions. The teacher who can describe movement in these terms has the vocabulary and necessary concepts to guide children as they learn.

INTRODUCING THE LESSON: INITIAL EXPLORATIONS

Explorations, the first moments in an expressive movement lesson, serve many purposes. They are used to set the tone or atmosphere of the class and establish an educational purpose. They are a natural place to prepare the children for creative activities by direct teaching. They can also be used to clarify language and movement concepts, gradually building up a movement vocabulary.

Beginning explorations should also be used to help children try out ways they can move their bodies. If the movement lesson calls for traveling and working with children who are learning to use space effectively, the first part of the activity could be used to emphasize the safe use of space. If the teacher plans to teach a lesson that involves running and leaping, the children might be introduced to explorations of jumps. In each case, the connection between movement and the language arts should be emphasized by introducing any new words which can be defined or clarified through movement. For instance, before a lesson in "Hist Whist" (lesson 4, chapter 7), the teacher may explain to the class that words like *hob-a-nob* and *ooch* sound like the actions they suggest and that the movement should reflect the sounds of the words.

During this phase of a lesson the children also expand their movement vocabulary (learn to perform increasingly complex movements) and learn to work toward high quality. The teacher may emphasize placing real effort behind a movement, concentrating on an action, or moving with greater sensitivity. Children will not achieve quality movement without patient help from an understanding adult. The separate exploratory actions are later combined to make movement sequences.

DEVELOPING MOVEMENT SEQUENCES

Our explorations are next combined in sequences, a group of actions occurring one after the other. Sequences may be compared to written sentences. If one thinks of a single action as a word, two or more actions put together become a "movement sentence" or sequence. To write sentences we need a vocabulary of words; to perform movement sentences we need a movement vocabulary, movement skills which we can perform.

As a first step in developing a movement sequence, the teacher writes a few evocative words on the blackboard. Each describes a single action and suggests *how* and *where* it is performed. In the following words, all the selections together highlight contrasting images that give an immediate picture of strength, speed, and level:

whirl	drift	explode
slither	dart	crumple
crawl	grip	shake

Lessons will be most successful if the children can define the words in movement terms and clarify both movement and language concepts through guided discussion. For example, the teacher may pose problems like:

1. Find a word in the list that suggests slow and low action.
2. Find a word that is strong and forceful and high.

3. Find two words that describe light actions and that can be used at any level.

Taking words from the list, we link any two contrasting words like *grip* and *shake*, performing one after the other. The sequence can be lengthened or shortened by adding more words, by performing each word a number of times in different ways, and by combinations of these two variations.

Building a Three-Word Sequence

We start developing a sequence with directions from the teacher, who asks the children to try out movements for several words, which are grouped together in many different ways after each movement is explored.

WE START WITH OUR EXPLORATIONS OF *GRIP*
1. Grip or clench your fists so tightly that your knuckles become white (only part of the body is used; see figure 1).
2. Push against the floor very hard with both hands (the children must feel actual resistance).
3. Which part of the body helped to push? (Make sure that every part of the body is involved.)
4. From a standing position, grip with every part of your *whole body* so that you feel that same tension in all your muscles, from toes up to face and neck (the whole body is included).

WE EXTEND EXPLORATIONS TO INCLUDE SHAKE
1. Shake one hand, then the other (naming different parts of the body one at a time).
2. Shake both hands really loosely . . . add one foot . . . now your head (leading up to action of the whole body; see figure 2).

WE COMBINE THE TWO ACTIONS
1. When I bang the tambourine, grip with any *part* of the body.
2. Now there will be three bangs. Each time there is a bang, you must grip in a different place or with a different part of you.
3. Shake all or different parts of your body each time there is a bang on the tambourine.

Figure 1. *Grip*—a boy uses considerable force clenching his fists.

WE ADD ANOTHER WORD, CRUMPLE
1. When I bang the tambourine, make your head flop . . . your head and shoulders (only part of the body is used).
2. This time crumple above your waist. Don't collapse right to the floor. Let your arms and head hang loosely (see figure 3).

WE PUT THE THREE WORDS TOGETHER TO FORM A COMPLETE SEQUENCE

After we have explored some of the possibilities provided by the sequence, we must decide on the duration of each part of the movement so that our sequence has form and clarity. When we know exactly what we want to do, we should be able to repeat it exactly. The following pattern is an example of a sequence that can be repeated:

Figure 2. *Shake*—a group of children shake both hands and feet.

1. Three gripping actions (using different parts of the body)
2. Shaking (the whole body)
3. Crumpling (the whole body)

There are many other ways we can put our sequence together. We could alter the sequence by making a pattern like *grip, shake, grip, shake, grip, shake, crumple.* The first two actions could be repeated two times in sequence to make *grip, grip, shake, shake, crumple.* There are numerous other possibilities.

Figure 3. *Crumple*—the children make their upper torsos "flop."

Because each action requires a different amount of effort, the three words—*grip*, *shake*, *crumple*—contrast strength and lightness. Actions using parts of the body also contrast with actions using the whole body, as can action which "travels" with "on the spot" action.

Let us choose three different words from our initial "vocabulary." Imagine the movement that might result from:

WHIRL   PAUSE   EXPLODE

We still have contrast in effort, but we have now chosen words that allow the children to move or travel across the floor (*whirl*) in contrast to the jump that will take place on the spot (*explode*). If we perform a sequence made up of whirling and exploding, we will need to slow down the forward momentum of the whirling so that energy can be directed to the upward thrust of the explosive jump. A *pause* will act as an ideal link between the two actions while momentarily stopping the flow of action and highlighting a contrast in movement. Like the preceding sequence, we can develop this one in a number of ways by exploring, selecting, and repeating different segments, practicing and refining what we wish to do.

Sequence Vocabulary

Primary teachers should select the words for their children to explore and build the movement vocabulary slowly with an emphasis on traveling actions. In the intermediate grades an "instant" movement vocabulary that also ensures movement contrast can be gathered by the whole class from the lists shown in Table 2. A separate heading for "travel" words encourages children to move from one area to another in some part of their sequence. Otherwise all actions might be localized in one area of the floor.

Table 2. Movement Vocabulary Providing for Contrast

Strong Action Words		*Light Action Words*	
thrust	explode	drift	float
kick	bound	flick	hover
slash	wring	dab	melt
press	pull	tremble	glide
		shake	slither

Words Describing Travel		*On-the-Spot Action Words*	
leap	creep	melt	expand
bound	crawl	ooze	vibrate
fly	reel	shrink	wobble
swirl	glide	shiver	sink
dart	lurch		

Words with No Movement	
freeze	pause
grip	balance

The children themselves can collect the action words, listing them on the blackboard. However, if the teacher initiates a discussion suggesting examples of action, the class will think of words more rapidly. Talking about a fighting scene will help children collect strong action words; discussion about birds and animals will help them collect words that suggest light, traveling movement.

These words can then be used for movement exploration by the group. Teachers will be most successful if they limit the words as follows:

1. Select two words, each from a different category, and combine them into a sequence.
2. Now extend your sequence by selecting another word or two from one or more of the other categories.

Regardless of how sequences are built, the children invariably learn the meanings of the words that are used. Thus, even in the process of designing dances they expand their vocabularies.

When Two or More Children Build a Sequence

Since boys and girls in the intermediate grades enjoy working with a partner or group, there is no reason why their first attempts at sequence building should not be a joint effort. Children need direct instruction, however, before they can use group work effectively. There are three techniques they should be taught: matching action, working in unison, and action/reaction.

MATCHING ACTION

When matching actions, children perform the same movements although not necessarily at the same time. *Mirroring* involves matching actions with opposite sides of the body and moving at exactly the same time as the partner (see figure 4). *Following and leading* is organized the same as a game of "follow the leader"; the follower has to observe carefully, and the leader has the responsibility of selecting the action.

WORKING IN UNISON

When children work in unison, action is synchronized or may be performed in succession (at different times). Children do not mirror

Figure 4. *Mirror action*—partners face each other and perform the same action with opposite sides of the body.

action on opposite sides of their bodies; rather, everyone moves the same side. A group running together across the room are running in unison (see figure 5).

ACTION/REACTION

In action/reaction, the child responds to a partner's or group's actions, but the response may be of a broad variety, broader than contrasts in mirror images. For instance, when members of a group collapse, they are acting. Their partners are reacting when they jump up at the same time, moving away (see figure 6).

GUIDING CHILDREN DURING THE LESSON

Once the children are working, the teacher observes and supervises the class, providing enough time for experimentation, guidance, and encouragement. Work will be more effective if the teacher uses the components of movement analysis, as discussed at the start of this

Figure 5. *Moving in unison*—a group of first-graders perform the same action.

chapter, in directions to the children: ***what***, ***where***, ***how***, and ***relationship***. In addition, the teacher must:

- Encourage the use of different parts of the body and the whole body.
- Stress differences in effort and speed so that the group becomes sensitive to how their bodies move.
- Observe the uses of space and help children become aware of direction and the levels on which they work.
- Encourage constructive use of relationships.

The teacher should also help the children develop sequences with a beginning, middle, and end. However short the pattern in an improvisation, sequences that give a sense of completion are more satisfying and promote an understanding of dance as an art. *Whirl, explode, crumple* for example, is a naturally dramatic sequence.

Even without a repeatable structure or a "beginning, middle, and end," many sequences developed from evocative action words can have dramatic impact. When boys are partners and words like *thrust, kick,* and *slash* are selected, mock fights frequently develop. If actual touching is not allowed, such "fights" are harmless. The fight has excellent movement potential, which can be broadened later through themes, poetry, and stories. In addition, vigorous, exhausting mock fight frequently dispels any notion that movement is effeminate.

Building sequences in this experimental manner has many other advantages. The children who work quickly can add to their patterns, making them more complex, while slower children work

Figure 6. *Action/reaction*—responding to her partner's action, a girl reacts in a broadly different way.

without pressure. Children quickly see that there is no "correct" solution for movement problems, since no two people produce the same sequence from the same words. Each person's ideas are valid and acceptable. The individualized approach helps children who are fearful of participating to develop confidence.

DEVELOPING MOVEMENT COMPOSITIONS FROM LITERATURE

Action words or sequence building may come from literary selections, as well as from randomly collected verbs. Poetry is especially suited to movement because it is compact and vivid, but a story may be treated in a similar way.

When a Poem or Story Has Action Words

Sometimes a poem will provide enough action words to give us all the sequence-building material we need. The following short poem is an example:

> Like a leaf or a feather
> In the windy, windy weather
> We will whirl around
> And turn around
> And all sink down
> Together.

—Anon.

STEP ONE

Read the poem. Then identify and discuss the main theme (the actions of the leaves in the wind).

STEP TWO

Extract the most important action words (*whirl, turn, sink*).

STEP THREE

Find ways to contrast and explore these actions using the movement analysis as a guide. (**What**? **How**? **Where**? With what **relationship**?)

STEP FOUR

Develop a sequence from the above. Decide upon the duration of each action, as well as starting and finishing positions.

STEP FIVE

Select the most effective accompaniment—the words themselves? percussion? sound effects? music? Consider suitability of lighting effects. (The use of light and sound in movement lessons is discussed in chapter 3.)

STEP SIX

Practice, observe others, and refine.

When More Action Words Must Be Supplied

Other literary selections are a little more challenging because the reader must supply some of his own action words in response to mood and imagery:

The Wind Has Wings[2]

Nunaptigne . . . In our land — *ahe, ahe, ee, ee, iee* —
The wind has wings, winter and summer.
It comes by night and it comes by day,
And children must fear it — *ahe, ahe, ee, ee, iee.*
In our land the nights are long,
And the spirits like to roam in the dark.
I've seen their faces, I've seen their eyes.
They are like ravens, hovering over the dead,
Their dark wings forming long shadows,
And children must fear them — *ahe, ahe, ee, ee, iee.*
                    Eskimo chant translated by
                    RAYMOND DE COCCOLA *and* PAUL KING

STEP ONE: FIND THE MAIN IDEA

The Eskimo wind, which is described in the poem as frightening, is compared with evil spirits that are like ravens hovering over

---

[2]Permission to reprint copyrighted poems presented in this book is acknowledged in the front pages.

the dead. We select as our main theme for movement: the frightening, evil wind.

STEP TWO: RECORD IMPORTANT ACTION WORDS

Which action words express the main idea of the poem? Some possibilities are *hover* and *roam*. In the case of *hover*, we have a light action word, a shape that may be menacing and movement that may take place on the spot (without traveling). Because we have chosen to emphasize the wind as frightening and evil, we ignore *roam* altogether.

STEP THREE: CREATE ACTION WORDS

In the absence of other descriptive action words, we must create our own, making sure that the words are in keeping with the theme of the poem—the evil, frightening wind. This search for words, which is later important for work in language arts, is most easily managed in two separate stages, a brainstorming session and a discussion in which verbs are extracted from the list that has been brainstormed.

In the *brainstorming* session, the children provide any word that is connected in their minds with the imagery in the poem. Although many words and phrases suggested will be synonyms, all must be accepted to encourage self-confidence and involvement. All will later be useful in creative writing. The following list came from a fifth–sixth grade class, to describe *the wind*:

strong	never-ceasing
evil	bird of prey
harsh	eagle
cold	soaring
cutting	dark
relentless	frightening

In the *discussion*, we divide the list into two parts, verbs and all other words. Only the verbs will be used; *cutting* indicates an action but "eagle" or "dark" does not. We can, however, add action words that describe our nouns. The children will quickly understand the difference. Our action words now are *cutting, soaring, never-ceasing,* which do not suggest the theme of the poem. We will need to find others that capture the feeling of the poem. The imagery of *bird of prey* suggests *clawing, twisting, tearing*. The imagery of a soaring, flying wind-bird suggests *running* and *leaping*. Our fifth–sixth grade class agreed on these five words, divided into two sequences:

claw	run
tear	leap
twist	

STEP FOUR: EXPLORATION AND CONTRAST

The first sequence—*claw, tear, twist*—is explored by three children working together while they stay in one place, on the spot, making shapes with their hands and moving their hands and arms with strong motions. Later, the sequence is varied by using action at different levels and in strong, sudden movements of the whole body "on-the-spot." In contrast to all the first actions which took place without traveling, the second sequence emphasizes running and leaping by children working without partners or the group. Uses of space, changes in speed, and a variety of leaps are explored.

STEP FIVE: START AND FINISH

The children work on starting and finishing positions, making their own choices.

STEP SIX: ACCOMPANIMENT

An accompaniment is chosen (cymbals scraped and clashed loudly for the first sequence, a loud drumming and beating played rhythmically for the running and leaping).

STEP SEVEN: DURATION

The duration of each action is selected. The children practice the movements so that they become familiar enough with the action to repeat it within a given duration.

STEP EIGHT: FINAL DEVELOPMENT

The children practice and refine their dance. The room is darkened except for a few flashlights, with shadows thrown against the walls. The lesson is performed in the darkened room with half the class acting as the audience while the other half interpret the selection. Later they change places.

GENERAL MANAGEMENT

Standards of Behavior

To ensure success in movement lessons, it is important to set clear standards of behavior, cooperation, and effort from the outset. Children must be made to realize that movement is a school subject with an educational purpose, just like arithmetic or reading. Everyone must clearly understand that a quiet tap on a drum or softly spoken "stop" must produce an instant "freeze." Children need to know the purpose of the movement lesson as much as they need to know the purpose of an arithmetic lesson. Careful lesson plans with no more than two teaching objectives will give the class a sense of purpose. The children are more likely to view movement as a serious school business if the teacher takes a few minutes of the start of each lesson to explain the purpose of the activities to take place. A statement at the end of the lesson summarizing what has been learned will further emphasize movement as a learning activity.

Observation

During the lesson teachers are dependent on skills of observation. Scrutinizing many children on the move in a large space can be difficult, but teachers can become skillful with practice, particularly when experience tells them what the outcomes of each activity will probably be.

Frequently directions can be given to children as they sit in a group close to the teacher. From this position, the children's faces will quickly reveal what they understand. Once the class is scattered around the room or on the move, teachers must continue to watch facial expressions to gain information, at the same time asking themselves the following questions:

- Are the children performing the task?
- Are they enjoying themselves?
- Are there any significant behavior problems?

If there are no immediate reasons to stop the class and redirect activity, teachers are free to watch, closely following one or two children for detailed information and gathering immediate impressions that will later be used as points of emphasis in the lesson.

If observations and explanations to the class are made in consistent movement terms (the *what, where, how* and *relationship* of movement), teaching will be more successful. For example the teacher who notices that the children are not putting enough effort into an action, discusses what they must do in terms of *how* the body moves (move with firm, strong action). Movement concepts thus become *guides for teaching*, as well as for lesson planning.

Demonstration

Children usually enjoy showing their ideas to the rest of the class. They also learn from watching each other and from listening to the teacher's comments. However, it is best to limit demonstrations because too many slow down the pace of the class (children lose interest). One workable method is to have two or three children show their sequences. Another is to have half the class watch the other half, later changing places. The second method offers numerous benefits:

- The teacher has fewer children to observe.
- The children can observe a variety of responses to a given task; gradually, observational skills of all the children improve.
- The teacher can guide observation by the children and establish a supportive atmosphere.
- The working group have more space.
- The working group, knowing that they are being observed, put greater care and effort into the activity.
- Groups can rest while watching, a break that will be very much in order if movement is vigorous.

Clothing

In movement lessons children should wear as few clothes as possible. Activity is often so energetic that, for their enjoyment and sense of freedom, the best choice is physical education clothes. When shorts and shirts are out of the question, a good compromise may be light T-shirts and bare feet, which produce a sensitivity to movement not possible with shoes.

Where Movement Classes Are Held

Perhaps the best place in school for expressive movement is the gym, where there is plenty of room for running and jumping. But many other locations are also suitable for movement lessons. On a pleasant, warm day the school playground provides a spacious setting. In some schools there may be space where others will not be disturbed in the instructional materials center or an empty hall. Movement lessons can also be easily carried out in the ordinary classroom if the children push the desks against the wall. Half the class sits on the desks while the other half improvises a dance. Even a classroom with bolted-down desks can be used if the teacher gives some thought to the kinds of movement children could do in a limited space.

Wherever movement takes place, the teacher should start the lesson by gathering the children around for a discussion. As the group talks, the teacher records important ideas on a blackboard or a large sheet of newsprint. The children then quickly scatter around the available empty space, exploring different movements and later improvising sequences. Any follow-up discussion can also take place in the same area, with the children gathered around the teacher once more.

SUMMARY

Lessons in expressive movement can be divided into several parts: an introductory activity or movement exploration, sequence building, and final development or improvisation.

Explorations ensure that every lesson gets off to a good start. The teacher considers the time, place, and previous activity. After the lunch hour, opening activities should be made for pent-up energies. Explorations stress careful use of space, running, stopping suddenly, bringing in all elements of movement (*what*, *where*, *how* and *relationships*). Later sequence building is developed from initial explorations. Introductory activities set the tone for the rest of the lesson, emphasizing attentive listening and controlled use of energy.

During explorations, movement concepts are introduced and experienced in an effort to help children understand them. Action words from which sequences are developed may be supplied by the children or found in a literary selection, but the teacher must clarify the concepts as the children work. Clarification may mean emphasis on variation, ways to repeat a sequence so that it is always of the same duration, or numerous other possibilities. The exploratory phase is important because quality of work depends on it. A push that has no real effort behind it is meaningless. A sudden darting action that is half-hearted will not give observer or performer a feeling of speed. Effort, concentration, and sensitivity in movement are not achieved instantly. Teachers will have to work for quality movement, by helping the children practice, and be prepared to wait for it.

The exploratory movements are next combined into sequences that are developed from a few evocative words, each of which describes an action. The children define the words through discussion and movement. They then decide on the duration of each part of the movement so that the sequence has form and clarity and so that they can repeat it exactly. Sequences may be developed by one, two, or more children working alone or together. They may use as stimulus word sequences developed either in the abstract or as representing a literary selection. Some of the children can later demonstrate their ideas to the group.

Throughout the lesson the teacher is careful to observe one or more of the children while they listen to directions, while they are on the move. Important things to watch for: Are the children performing the intended task? Are they enjoying it? Are there significant behavior problems?

In the final development, the group is concerned with completing and summarizing the work in the lesson. There is an immediate return to the idea or story that may have been put aside during sequence building and exploration. Particular attention is given to accompaniment and lighting. Some or all of the children's own ideas come into play. After some experience with movement, they may even have full responsibility for the summation.

The concluding part of the lesson will be most satisfying if the children have gained a sense of mastery over their movement through ample practice. With younger children practice may be relatively short. With children in the intermediate grades, a movement composition may take several weeks to complete, allowing opportunities for ideas to formulate and for integration with other related classroom activities like creative writing or critical reading.

BIBLIOGRAPHY: SOURCES ON DESIGNING MOVEMENT LESSONS

Boorman, Joyce. *Creative Dance in the First Three Grades*. Don Mills, Ont.: Longmans, 1969.

Boorman, Joyce. *Creative Dance in Grades Four to Six*. Don Mills, Ont.: Longmans, 1971.

Exiner, Johanna, & Lloyd, Phyllis. *Teaching Creative Movement*. New York: Plays, Inc., 1973.

Laban, Rudolph. *Modern Educational Dance*. London: MacDonald and Evans, 1963.

North, Marion. *A Simple Guide to Movement Teaching*. Exeter, Eng.: Wheaton, 1965.

North, Marion. *Composing Movement Sequences*. Exeter, Eng.: Wheaton, 1965.

Russell, Joan. *Creative Dance in the Primary School*. London: McDonald and Evans, 1965.

Russell, Joan. *Creative Dance in the Secondary School*. London: McDonald and Evans, 1965.

Shreeves, Rosamund. *Movement and Educational Dance for Children*. Boston: Plays, Inc., 1979.

3

Planning Light and Sound Effects

WHY USE LIGHT AND SOUND EFFECTS?

Imagine a darkened room lit with a few bright spots of light here and there. The children are interpreting "Hist Whist" (lesson 4, chapter 7), whispering "hist whist" and "ghost things" as they move. They are carried away as the "ghost things" seem to become phantoms, the "great devil" menacing with larger-than-life shadows. The members of the group relax their guard and abandon themselves to the sensory experience as the sound of their voices adds to the dramatic impact of the action, becoming at the same time a guide for tempo and mood. The result is twofold. Movement is improved, and light and sound effects combine to make the lesson memorable.

This chapter contains basic information on how to use light and sound as aids in the movement class. It includes lists of light and sound effects that may be bought or made easily, guides to using them, and specific suggestions for their use. Percussion instruments, verbal sounds, tape recorder sounds, and musical selections are discussed in the section on sound effects. Flashlights, colored floodlights, fluorescent strips, strobe lights, and mini-flashlights are treated in the section on light effects.

SOUND EFFECTS

Percussion Instruments

Percussion instruments, the simplest and most effective instrumental accompaniment, include tambourines, drums, cymbals, gongs, castanets-on-a-stick, maracas, hand sounds, and a variety of "found" objects. All provide opportunities for banging, shaking, clanging and scraping. Compared to a complex instrument, the piano, for example, most percussion instruments produce primitive sounds. But the beat of these simple instruments can be very satisfying when combined with movement, particularly since children can accompany themselves or each other. Furthermore, when a variety of percussion instruments are used, there are opportunities for the creative use of sound and for surprising effects with considerable range of sound. As a result, percussion is excellent for teaching movement and for encouraging children to listen, remember, and respond to simple rhythms and evocative sounds.

Some of the conventional kinds of percussion instruments can be made very successfully by both primary- and intermediate-grade children, who always enjoy a "do-it-yourself" percussion project. Simple instructions for making a tom-tom drum, button castanets, shakers, and maracas are given in the appendix to this chapter.

THE TAMBOURINE

The great virtue of the tambourine is that it is two instruments in one. It can be shaken as well as banged or tapped, combining some of the qualities of a drum and of maracas. Shaking a tambourine is an excellent way to guide children in light, quick movement or light, sustained actions, as in "Visit" (lesson 9, chapter 6). When shaking and banging are combined, the teacher can guide the children while they travel and halt, developing sequences on the spot.

Loud, firm bangs made with the hand or a drum stick will encourage strong actions or distinct rhythm. Rubbing or tapping the surface with finger tips will create a harder patter, which is particularly suited to "Rain" (lesson 3, chapter 6). An excellent place to use a scraping sound as accompaniment is "Visit."

THE DRUM

The drum is a highly adaptable instrument ranging in intensity from soft and soothing to loud and excitable. Because a variety of moods are evoked with changes in speed and volume, the drum is excellent for lessons emphasizing *how* the body moves. It is also ideal for beating out rhythm patterns suitable for walking, running, skipping, and waltz time. "Wild Iron" (lesson 5, chapter 7) is one of many lessons in which the drum may be used to advantage.

Sounds may be made on the drum in a variety of ways—tapping with the padded end of a drumstick, tapping or scraping with the tip of the drumstick on the flat surface or rim of the drum, "scratching" the surface of the drum with the fingernails. The last two sounds are suited to small, light movements.

CYMBALS

Cymbals create a strident clang that fills the air, lingering a moment or two before fading away. The cymbal, therefore, is ideal for any action that drifts or dies away slowly, particularly for strong actions like leaping or thrusting. A drumstick used with a cymbal will produce a continuous, metallic rumbling if the stick is run back and forth along the surface of the cymbal. Quickly jabbing the tip of the stick against the surface will produce a harsher, sudden sound. Rubbing two cymbals together will make a scraping sound that is ideal for strong, flowing movement.

GONG

The gong (sometimes called the Chinese gong) is a metal drum suspended by a string. Combining the sounds of cymbals and drum, it handles like a drum.

CASTANETS

Individual castanets are difficult to play with control; but when attached to a stick, they require only a firm shake. Excellent for quick, sudden action, when shaken vigorously they produce a series of short, explosive, rather high-pitched sounds. Although they do not produce a variety of sounds, intensity can be varied, adding considerably to an activity.

MARACAS

The sounds made by maracas are not unlike those of a tambourine and are excellent for light movement, either continuous or with a pulsating beat. Maracas are relatively inexpensive to buy; they can also be made successfully by children.

"FOUND" OBJECTS

All sorts of objects found around a school can be used as percussion instruments. Rulers are useful for beating out rhythms when tapped, rapped or scraped against the floor, walls, or classroom furniture. Rings of keys are good substitutes for castanets. Other useful "found" objects include shoes, wood blocks, dowels of wood, and bottles filled with varying amounts of liquid. When using hard-soled shoes, children can create a hard sound by hitting the heels together. Hitting a shoe heel against the floor will create a drumming sound. Bottles holding different amounts of water will make varying tones. Children enjoy experimenting with all these objects, as well as others they may find.

HAND SOUNDS

One can make hand sounds in a number of ways. Clapping hands against each other creates a rather sudden, sharp, emphatic sound. Snapping one finger against another makes a light, popping sound. Hitting the fingernails against the floor or another hard object produces a tapping sound; hitting the flat of the hand against the floor, a thumping sound. Children enjoy inventing "conversations" after experimenting with the possibilities. For example:

1. "A" claps, snaps, or drums a simple rhythm. "B" echoes it.
2. "A" claps, snaps, or drums a rhythm, and "B" answers using a different hand sound.
3. "A" and "B" "talk," alternately using contrasting sounds (for instance, sustained sounds and quick, light sounds).

Verbal Sounds

The voice is also an excellent instrument for sound effects that suggest quick, slow, flowing, and/or broken movements. Ways to use it are described here under the following headings: Alphabet Sounds, Mood Sounds, Single Words and Phrases, Choral Reading.

ALPHABET SOUNDS

Children often use alphabet sounds spontaneously when they are working together on a movement sequence, particularly if the class is accustomed to percussion accompaniment. Classes working on "Fireworks" (lesson 7, chapter 7) sometimes respond to "rocket" movements with "sh-sh-sh" sounds. Consonants like "b," "ch," "k," and "t" repeated over and over again produce a series of light, explosive sounds, like "ch-ch-ch," which some children spontaneously voice to accompany "Fireworks." Vowel sounds can also be used to create a background for movement, setting the mood as well as the tempo. Some groups performing "The Wind Has Wings" have accompanied their dance with the vowel sounds of its refrain, to create a wind-like sound. Classes have used "ah-ah-ah-ah" to express delight after the explosion in "Fireworks." In mirror games, many children enjoy "speaking" to each other while using vowels only.

MOOD SOUNDS

Many voiced sounds that are not necessarily alphabetical can be particularly exciting in movement activities. Possibilities include sighing, groaning, a witch's cackle, sobbing, shouting, whistling, hushing. Bird whistles are excellent for "Ducks' Ditty" (lesson 4, chapter 6); whistling sounds like police whistles for "Traffic," (exploration 2, chapter 5); sighing and shouting for "Get Up, Blues" (lesson 2, chapter 7). Car sounds are also a great addition to "Traffic."

SINGLE WORDS AND PHRASES

Repeating a particular word over and over again is also an effective accompaniment for movement, for instance, repeating words like *whisper* or *softly*, both of which contain a sibilant—words like *ghost things* or *hist whist* are ideally suited for accompanying movement to "Hist Whist." Words with consonants like "b" (burst) or "x" (explode) are excellent as accompaniment for leaps and jumps. The children literally shout the word as they jump. Sometimes two or three words can be sequenced to create a rhythm that suggests certain movement without necessarily making sense. For example:

SPLAT, SPLASH, platter, platter, platter, platter
WHAM, BAM, CLING, CLANG
Cinderella, Cinderella, Pumpkin pie

Verbal sounds like these suggest action sequences and provide rhythmic accompaniment.

Sometimes the words may be delivered in chorus to create a textured quality. Any words may be used for this purpose, whether taken from the children themselves or an outside source. In an exploration in which they "invented" a hamburger-making machine, a class recited TV ads for MacDonald hamburgers, in three parts. Group 1 repeatedly recited: "Two all-beef patties, special sauce, lettuce, cheese, pickles, onions on a sesame seed bun." A second group chanted, at spaced intervals, "The Big Mac attack!" A third group periodically sang, "MacDonald's!" using a melody they had heard on television. (The scheme is represented graphically in Table 3.) The resulting *verbal obbligato* was amusing and very effective.

CHORAL READING

Group recitation can also provide an excellent accompaniment or introduction to a movement composition. Short extracts or even a complete poem, if not too long, can provide meaning and rhythm as a spoken accompaniment whether "live" (recited by the children during movement) or taped.

Usually literary choral selections are used with movement in one of the following ways:

- As an introduction to movement
- As accompaniment to movement
- With choral selection and movement alternating

When movement accompanies the choral selection, the children can chant the words while they are moving, or the group can be divided into two parts with some moving and the others reciting the selection.

Table 3. Verbal Obbligato for "MacDonald's Machine"

Group 1	Group 2	Group 3
Two all-beef patties,	The Big Mac attack!	MacDonald's!
special sauce,		MacDonald's!
lettuce, cheese,		MacDonald's!
pickles, onions	The Big Mac attack!	MacDonald's!
on a sesame seed bun.		

Using choral reading for sound effects with movement has many advantages. Children who read well help their less proficient classmates by setting a reasonable pace and by reading in a meaningful way. New vocabulary, therefore, is more likely to be pronounced correctly and learned well. In addition, movement provides children with a natural way to absorb word meaning, because words are associated with experiences. As a result, the children understand more fully how to read aloud. They also achieve better reading comprehension and broader language arts abilities.

Traditionally, voices are classified as light (high) and dark (low), but at the elementary school level such arrangements are impossible because young children's voices are uniformly light. Therefore, the class must be divided in other ways, perhaps with boys in one group and girls in another. The class may also be arbitrarily divided into small groups. Interesting effects can be achieved by placing groups of children in different parts of the room, from where they project their voices in whispers, shouts, or normal tones.

Traditionally, choral performances have also been concerned with quality of performance, but a finished effect cannot be expected from young children. Stray voices frequently straggle in after the rest of the group has stopped, tempo falters, poems are read in a sing-song fashion. It is important that teachers accept the imperfections of young choral readers, making efforts at improvement only for limited objectives. The children will enjoy reading much more if it is done in a relatively uncritical atmosphere. If work must be halted because the class is not reading together, the teacher can point out the problem by replaying the reading on a tape recorder and asking for pupil criticism. The offenders will soon hear their voices trailing others. A similar approach is useful when the class reads in a sing-song fashion.

In planning a choral reading, teachers or children should ask themselves these questions:

- What is the subject of the poem?
- What is its mood?
- What is the best tempo for this selection?
- Where is the climax?
- Is there any place where this poem should change dramatically during the reading?

- Should the poem be presented so that everyone always speaks together or should it be divided into parts?
- Are there any special sound effects that will heighten the experience? For instance, should parts of the poem be louder or softer? Should vowels be emphasized? Should some or all of the consonants be precisely stated?

The answers are not necessarily the same for every group preparing the same selection, and the choices made can mean a difference in dramatic impact.

Here is an example of the line of reasoning teacher and children should follow in deciding what to do. Suppose the group plans to interpret "The Wind Has Wings," highlighting the mood emphasized in the movement lesson described in chapter 2—fear of the wind. After answering the preliminary questions, they decide on three guidelines.

1. The lines expressing fear should emphasize vowels and sibilants elongating the words, so that they sound fearful. Therefore, the pace will be relatively slow.
2. To contrast the sound further, the howl of the wind and words expressing fear should be divided into at least two parts.
3. Lines 6–9 should be the climax of the poem. In some way these may be set off from the rest of the poem.

The group or the teacher now designs several choral plans, in terms of how the group could divide for reading parts of the poem. (See, for example, the plans shown in Table 4.) All the plans are tried out, and one is selected as preferred.

There are many ways to arrange a poem for a chorus. The simplest calls for all the children to read in unison—"Peter White" (lesson 1, chapter 6) is an example of a poem suited to such a rendition. In another simple arrangement, sometimes dubbed "line-a-child," that is used often in elementary schools each child speaks one line—"Seesaw" (lesson 2, chapter 6) lends itself to an interpretation along such lines. Elementary-grade children can also handle changes in pace: note that several selections in chapter 6 can be read quickly

Table 4. Three Choral Plans for "The Wind Has Wings"

Plan 1	Plan 2	Plan 3	
Group 1	All	All	*Nunaptigne*[1] . . . In our land — *ahe, ahe, ee, ee, iee* —
Group 2	Child 1	Solo	The wind has wings, winter and summer. It comes by night and it comes by day,
Group 1	All	All	And children must fear it — *ahe, ahe, ee, ee, iee.*
Group 2	Child 2	Solo	In our land the nights are long,
Solo with wailing background[2]	Child 3 Child 4 Child 5 *(softly)* Child 6	Solo with whispered background[3]	And the spirits like to roam in the dark. I've seen their faces, I've seen their eyes. They are like ravens, hovering over the dead, Their dark wings forming long shadows,
Group 1	All	All	And children must fear them — *ahe, ahe, ee, ee, iee.*

[1]Pronounced (probably): Noo-nap-teenya.
[2]Background: vowel sounds (those of the refrain, or perhaps "ooh. . . ."). The sounds of the refrain could be: Ah-ay, ah-ay, ee, ee, ah-ee.
[3]Background: lines of the poem, or selected words whispered at intervals.

at the beginning and slowly at a later point, or vice versa (for example, "Song of the Train" and "A Lazy Thought.") These arrangements work well for both primary- and intermediate-grade children. Combinations of them can produce interesting choral effects that even the youngest children can handle easily and create with the teacher's help and guidance.

Tape Recorder

Choral and other sounds may, of course, be recorded on tape. The tape recorder can also produce its own exciting array of sound effects by simply changing speed. Deep, prolonged sounds are produced when the tape is played at slow speed; high pitched squeaks emerge at fast speed. When percussion, verbal sounds, and other sound

effects are subjected to speed distortion, the results are often
humorous or bizarre, and always surprising. They can also be an excellent accompaniment for movement.

Music

If well chosen, music is probably the most stimulating and emotionally satisfying accompaniment for movement whether it is live,
on records, or on cassette tapes. Of the two ways to reproduce
music, tapes are preferable because records are expensive. The
careful teacher, for very little cost, can gradually collect selections
and have them ready for movement activities. Excerpts are probably
better than complete selections because a class of children can only
dance for a limited time, usually somewhere between thirty seconds
and two minutes.

Selecting music is essentially a matter of individual preference.
However, the following records have proved useful and can be
recommended.

POP

Barry, John. *John Barry Conducts His Own Greatest Hits*, Columbia,
CS9508.

Diamonds Are Forever (sound track). United Artists, ULK3015.

Goldfinger (sound track). United Artists, UAS5117.

Anderson, LeRoy. *Sound of LeRoy Anderson: Ping Pong Percussion by
Stradivari Strings.* Pirouette, FRMB2.

Mary Poppins (sound track). Buena Vista, S4026.

The Good, the Bad and the Ugly (sound track). United Artists, VAS5112.

West Side Story (sound track). Columbia, OS2070.

Mancini, Henry. *Pink Panther* (sound track). RCA, ANL1-1369.

Bolan, Mark, & Rex, T. *Electric Warrior.* RePrise, 6466.

Kingsley, Perry. *The In Sound from Way Out.* Vanguard, 79222.

Tomita. *Tomita's Greatest Hits.* RCA KRLI7074.

CLASSICAL

Copland, Aaron. *Appalachian Spring.* Leonard Bernstein and the New
York Philharmonic. Columbia, ML5755.

Debussy, Claude. *Afternoon of a Faun.* Leonard Bernstein and the New
York Philharmonic. Columbia, MS6754.

Dukas, Paul. *The Sorcerer's Apprentice.* Dimitri Mitropoulos and the New
York Philharmonic. Columbia, 5198.

Dvorak, Antonin. *Slavonic Dances.* Leonard Bernstein and the New York Philharmonic. Columbia, MS6879.

Gounod, Charles. "The Waltz" from *Faust. Invitation to the Waltz.* Angel, S3622.

Grieg, Edvard. "Anitra's Dance" and "In the Hall of the Mountain King," in *Peer Gynt Suite*, Op. 46, No. 1. Leonard Bernstein and the New York Philharmonic. Columbia, M31800.

Holst, Gustav. *The Planets.* Adrian Boult and the Birmingham Orchestra. Angel, S36420.

Ibert, Jacques. *Divertissement.* Martinon and the Paris Conservatory Orchestra. London, STS15093.

Mussorgsky, Modeste. *A Night on Bald Mountain.* Antal Dorati and the London Symphony. Mer 75025.

Rudolph Kempe Conducts Music from Czechoslovakia. Seraphim, S60098.

St. Säens, Claude. *Danse Macabre.* Eugene Ormandy and the Philadelphia Symphony. RCA, CRL30985.

Strauss, Richard. *Also Sprach Zarathustra.* Eugene Ormandy and the Philadelphia Symphony. Columbia, M31829.

LIGHT EFFECTS

Flashlights

The simplest way of producing a light effect is to use a few flashlights in a darkened room. If the lights are strong, three or four strategically placed flashlights can set an exciting stage for movement— "Visit" is well suited to a lighting arrangement with one or two flashlights placed around a room.

For a diffused, warmer light, flashlights can be placed inside a cover, like the red conical road markers used on the highways or the plastic pumpkins used at Halloween. Once the room is dark and flashlights are turned on, the outer covering is hard to identify, leaving a number of glowing red and orange objects on the floor. An arrangement with road markers is especially well suited to the witches' scenes from *Macbeth* (lesson 10, chapter 7).

Colored Floodlights

Colored two-hundred watt bulbs (the light bulbs used most frequently on house exteriors at Christmastime) produce diffused light in a variety of colors. When attached to a socket with a few feet of electrical cord and plugged into the wall, they can be used with considerable flexibility. The teacher directs the light so that it creates shadows on different walls and influences the way children use the floor space—"Visit" is very well suited to lighting with a single bulb.

Overhead Projector

An overhead projector throws a considerable amount of light into a darkened room. When covered with cinamoid, colored sheets of plastic material frequently used in the theater, possibilities for an infinite variety of colors open up. Projectors may also be used to throw images or pictures relevant to the story or movement idea against the wall. A cutout of a moon used with an overhead projector in a darkened room makes a good background for "Visit."

Fluorescent Strips

Strips of fluorescent materials with adhesive backing can be bought from a bicycle shop. When placed on clothing or on children's hands, aerial patterns will show up in the dark. Interesting effects can be achieved with fluorescent strips when the group moves in "Fireworks," or other selections interpreted in the dark.

Strobe Lights

Although strobe lights are expensive, purchasing or renting is sometimes worth while. The strong flicker effect of the strobe can seem to disembody a room full of active children. (It can be very effective with the lesson "Monster," in chapter 6.) But at high speed and in a darkened room, a strobe light can make children feel very dizzy. For this reason, strobes should not be used at the fast settings with primary classes, and they should be handled with care even in the intermediate grades.

Mini-Flashlights

Mini-flashlights, the very small flashlights that look like fat cigars, are the best value of all. They produce a very small, intense spot of light. When the entire class switches them on, bright individual spots—like stars—are seen all over the room. A number of movement concepts can be taught with these flashlights, including gestures used to make air patterns. By playing with the lights, the children can learn to create a variety of effects. When a flashlight is pointed up toward the ceiling, the beam spreads out over a good-sized area. When it is pointed toward the floor, a smaller area is lit. The children will make a diffused red glow if they put their fingers and the palm of one hand over the bulb. A quick zigzag action will produce a continuous line of light. There are numerous lessons and selections in chapters 6 and 7 with which the mini-flashlights can be useful, including "Hist Whist," "Fireworks," and "Visit."

SUMMARY

Light and sound effects add excitement and drama to movement lessons. The hand drum and tambourine are the most useful of the percussion instruments because they produce so many variations in speed, volume, and rhythm. Children enjoy using percussion instruments and making sound effects.

By far the best light effects are flashlights. They can be used in many situations, and are inexpensive. Overhead projectors and fluorescent strips are also easily available and inexpensive.

APPENDIX: DO-IT-YOURSELF PERCUSSION INSTRUMENTS

Tom-Tom Drum

You will need:

Large coffee can with a removable plastic lid

White paint

Tempera colors

Decorative paper with sticky side

Dowel stick

Bead with a hole big enough to slip in the dowel stick

Directions:

Remove the lid from the can. Put it aside.

Paint the can with the paint. Dry. Decorate with tempera colors and paper.

To make a drumstick, glue the dowel inside the bead.

Paint the drumstick and decorate.

When the drum is dry put the lid back on the can.

Button Castanets

You will need:
 Two buttons, same size
 3/4"-wide elastic
 Needle and thread

Directions:
 Cut two small pieces of elastic, just long enough to stretch securely around the child's thumb and index finger, respectively.
 Sew each piece of elastic into a loop.
 Choose two buttons and sew a loop to one side of each button.

Shakers

You will need:
 Small aluminum pie tins
 Tongue depressors (2)
 White glue diluted in water
 Stapler
 Dried beans, pebbles
 Tissue paper
 Tempera paint

Directions:
 Staple two pie tins together around the edges. Leave a space for filling the plate with beans and pebbles. Push in dried beans or pebbles.
 Glue 2 tongue depressors together. Push into the pie tin opening. Make sure the handle is secure by stapling them in place.
 Cover the tins with tissue paper or colored paper.
 Decorate the handle with tempera paint.

Maracas

You will need:
 A balloon
 Newspaper
 A stick or dowel, 1/4" in diameter and 5–6" long
 Flour

Water

Pebbles, dried beans, peas, rice or elbow macaroni

Directions:

Blow up a balloon to the size of a grapefruit.

Cover with papier mâché as follows:

Tear newspapers into strips about 1″ wide.

Mix flour and water to make paste.

Soak paper strips in paste.

Lay over balloon.

Let dry.

Punch two holes in papier mâché balloon.

Pour in pebbles or other dried objects.

Slide handle (a stick 1/4″ in diameter) through holes until it sticks out about 1/2″ on one side and 5-6″ on other side.

Glue stick to papier mâché and cover with more papier mâché.

Decorate the maracas with a colorful design.

4

Planning for Language Arts Objectives

OBJECTIVES OF THE LANGUAGE ARTS CURRICULUM

A few years ago a committee of the National Assessment of Educational Progress (NAEP) initiated a series of tests that could be used to evaluate the educational progress of American children at certain grade levels. Before the tests were designed and administered, the group agreed on general objectives for national education. In the area of language arts, their objectives included the following:[1]

1. Children should listen to literature.
2. Children should read, witness, and respond to literature in a variety of ways, sharing the response with others, recognizing social and personal values expressed in literature, responding emotionally and reflectively.
3. Children should be able to value reading, assess materials for readability, demonstrate word recognition skills in reading comprehension (literal and inferential), and use a variety of approaches in gathering information.
4. Children should have a variety of writing experiences.

Most authorities agree with these objectives, which research has shown foster language development, growth in reading, listening

---

[1]Summarized from *National Assessment and the Teaching of English*, ed. John C. Mellon (Urbana: National Council of Teachers of English, 1975), pp. 75-99.

skills, and writing. Because the expressive movement lessons in this book draw on oral language, literature, reading, and writing, the carefully designed lessons can help achieve many NAEP goals. Good planning for movement lessons should include considering ways to teach listening and reading skills and to help children expand vocabulary. In addition, teachers can use movement lessons to extend children's experience in creative drama, reading, and writing activities.

Vocabulary

Research has shown that children first grasp meaning by associating words with concrete experience. This continues to be true during the early and middle years in childhood. Since children actually associate firsthand experience with words during movement lessons, and since lessons are planned around selected words, vocabulary is learned incidentally without special planning. The teacher's directions affect how much and what kind of vocabulary is learned.

Fine differences in meaning are highlighted by tasks like the following:

Show what you do when you walk . . . stride . . . stroll . . . strut.

Actions clarify differences in meaning in the most unambiguous terms.

Several *meanings for a single word* can be explored in depth by presenting it in a variety of sentences and by asking the children to move as suggested:

They ran to the corner and back.
The ball ran over the curb and into the street.
The train ran along the track.
The ivy ran up the side of the building.
They ran goods across the border in a smuggling operation.

The meanings of *structure words* are explored as pupils work their way through various obstacles, as suggested by phrases like:

around the chair	*along* the line
over the box	*across* the line
under the table	*in* the square
with your friend	*on* the box
after your teacher	
before the clock	

Some other structure words that may be learned through movement are:

by	away
into	upon
from	down

Older boys and girls can also learn the meanings of abstract words like *fear*, *anxiety*, and *pleasure* through activities like:

Show me with your body that you are afraid.

How would you walk if you were afraid?
How would you sit?
How would you hold your hands?
Tell me other things you would do if you were afraid.

Listening

Because every movement lesson places many demands on children to listen and respond immediately to directions, explorations and improvisations are excellent for emphasizing thoughtful listening. The teacher's directions make the difference in quality of listening.

Children show that they are listening and can follow simple oral directions in tasks like:
Jump from one foot to the other.

Children show that they are listening and can remember significant details accurately with directions like:
Jump to a count of six and then run to a count of eight.

Children show that they are listening and can discriminate between the meanings of words with directions like:
Can you strut?
Can you amble?
Can you stroll?

Children listen and discriminate between the connotative meanings of words when they follow directions like:
I want you to strut (stride, limp, amble, etc.).
Show your feelings clearly in your body movement.

Children show that they can listen and follow the sequence of a story with tasks like:
I am going to read you a story.
I want you to pantomime it after I read it.

There are many advantages to teaching listening in the movement setting. The teacher knows immediately if the children have heard or understood because they respond immediately. The action and tasks themselves keep the children involved.

Reading

Although expressive movement lessons are not generally conceived as reading lessons, children's reading abilities are broadly affected. Often boys and girls have a chance to read orally in chorus, and reading comprehension is deepened. Even word recognition may be taught on occasion.

To teach almost any aspect of reading except choral reading (see chapter 3), only a little planning for reading need be done. For instance, word recognition may be taught by simply using written words, rather than oral ones, as cues for action. Teaching reading comprehension is equally simple. Many of the movement lessons translate verbal into concrete experience while emphasizing some aspect of the theme, the rhythm, the figurative language, or the mood of a literary selection. The teacher need only help the children discuss the ideas emphasized so that the group recall details, interpret the selection, compare their experiences with ones suggested in the poem, and evaluate the selection. Examples of some lessons designed to deepen comprehension may be found in chapters 6 and 7.

Discussion

The teacher can set the scene for higher level thinking with carefully planned questions, for quality of questions makes the difference between success and failure in teaching reflective thinking. After reading "The Wind Has Wings," the children will recall details of the poem with questions like the following:

What was afraid of the wind?
When is the speaker afraid of the wind?
What is the wind like?

The following questions will help the children interpret the poem:

Who is saying "ahe, ahe, ee, ee, iee"?
What do you think made the people afraid of the wind?
What do you suppose the wind did?

The children will apply Eskimo experience to their own if they have a chance to compare their own experiences with those suggested in the poem. Questions like the following will help them remember their own experiences and compare them with those of Eskimos.

Do you remember any time when there was a strong wind?
Have you ever been out in a wind storm?

The children will synthesize the elements of the poem in responding to suggestions like these:

Retell the poem from the point of view of the wind.

Make a sound effects tape of the wind.

Draw pictures of the land, pictures which will tell us why the wind is evil.

Write a poem about a different kind of wind, perhaps a breeze, a gusty fall wind, a tornado.

Older, more mature children will be led to analyze and evaluate the poem with questions and suggestions like:

What does the title mean?
Look for the words that paint the picture of the wind.
Look for the words and phrases that show the wind is dangerous.

The children will also be able to evaluate the poem if they have a chance to compare it with other poems about the same topic, for example:

Behn, Harry. "Windy Morning." In *Time for Poetry*, ed. by M. H. Arbuthnot & S. Root. New York: Scott, Foresman, 1968.
Rossetti, Christina. "Who Has Seen the Wind?" In *Every Child's Book of Verse*, ed. by Sara Chokla Gross. New York: Watts, 1968.

Creative response, plus effective questions and comparisons between literary selections, will help children read literature reflectively.

EXTENDING LESSONS TO OTHER FORMS OF EXPRESSION

Although not every lesson need be extended to other forms of expression, some seem to flow easily from one form to another. Such moments are valuable educationally, for they offer children further opportunities to express ideas. During movement lessons, the class experiences a story or poem at a preverbal or kinesthetic level. Play-acting (drama) or writing then offers the boys and girls a chance to verbalize the movement experience. Like the child who said, "How do I know what I think until I have said it?" extended activities allow children to express what they think and feel.

Creative Drama

Many movement lessons flow directly into the drama sessions through an exploration of the characters, setting, or plot of the story. Often a simple movement game may lead directly to drama. With guidance and a few ideas on characters, plot, and setting, the children soon devise their own story. For example, a group may try to explore a character's movement after questions like:

> You are walking down the street. How do you walk? Do you take big steps or shuffle along?

> Are you carrying something in your hand? Show me how heavy it is and how large it is.

Later, with the help of the teacher, the group develop a story around their character, deciding first where the story takes place and what happens.

Questions like the following will help children create a drama:

> What is your character's name?
> Where is your story taking place?
> What happens?

Mirroring also readily lends itself to drama. Two children follow each other around the room as the teacher suggests the following:

> One of you is the leader, the other the follower.

> Move very slowly. It is dark and you don't want to be seen. The second person is a cop, the first a robber.

> Move as stealthily as possible. Remember, you don't want to be seen.

> Robber, turn sharply. You want to turn the street corner to get away. The cop is catching up with you; so move quickly.

Even something as simple as an exploration of jumps may become a story by the addition of characters, setting, and conflict. For example, the teacher asks several children to form a box with their bodies:

Four or more of you form a box with your bodies.

Now each of you make your bodies as small as possible. When you hear my signal, jump as high as possible, staying together.

You are an elevator. Make your box look like an elevator. You are moving from the second to the fifth floor. Now go down to the first floor.

Some people are going to get on the elevator. There is a little old woman carrying a heavy shopping bag, a little girl with a bouncing ball, a man reading the evening paper.

Go up to the fifth floor.

Oh, oh. You are stuck on the third floor. What will the passengers do?

Older children enjoy exploring a variety of movements which express anger, fear, humiliation, pain, and sorrow. A dramatic scene is developed afterwards by setting the scene, naming the characters and suggesting a conflict:

You are angry. How do you hold your torso, your head, your arms?

Try looking angry while you stand, sit, fight.

Two of you are in a fight in the school yard. You are very angry because one of you has told the teacher a secret of the other.

What happens when the teacher comes into the yard?

The drama thus developed can be performed in a number of ways:

PANTOMIME

Groups without experience find pantomime drama easy because it often grows quite naturally out of movement. Storyline can be suggested by movement or a narrator can accompany the acting with a story.

STORIES WITH IMPROVISED DIALOGUE

In general, children handle oral language more effectively after some acting experience. The children often decide for themselves when they are ready to try dialogue by simply beginning to speak. A book with suggestions for introducing children to creative drama is *Development Through Drama*, by Brian Way (Longmans, 1963).

STORIES WITH WRITTEN DIALOGUE

When they have written scripts, children act in a more formal way. Many teachers like to use written plays because the children can write their own plays and because the script offers children opportunities to read aloud.

VARIATIONS ON THESE BASIC POSSIBILITIES

Stories may be acted around body shapes of children in tableaux, "pictures" posed by living people. Using static shapes, actors depict a dramatic situation or story, the postures they assume suggesting that something has just occurred or is just about to occur. Several scenes posed one after another in this way give the viewers a sense of story line. In each scene a dramatic suggestion of action revolves around a central figure or figures. Dramatic effects in tableaux are also achieved by lighting devices like spotlights, by placing frames around an entire scene, or silhouetting the entire "picture" behind a sheet. Another interesting way to dramatize a story is to have the children act out the parts behind a sheet with a spotlight placed in back of them. Children also enjoy reading a script or narrating a story while actors move through the action.

Writing: Word Pictures from Movement Pictures

Of all the ways to extend movement experiences, writing is often the most satisfying. Written sentences using words from movement sentences (sequences) seem a natural extension of improvisation. Frequently, the children are carried away with "painting pictures" with their bodies and with words. The excitement that is so often a part of movement lessons is carried over to creative writing so that children write "intensely." As a result, the writing often reflects an intuitive grasp of form and stronger use of language.

The best possible way to approach writing after movement is as follows: The teacher guides the children through a movement sequence using action words. Later, the same words are used in creative writing. A variation of this approach grows out of a "happening" (simulation using light and sound effects) which the children develop for a movement sequence. Light and sound effects together with the action help release the imagination as the fantasy the children create flows into their writing.

As the children create a movement sequence from action words, the teacher helps them understand that they are painting "movement pictures." Later the same words are used for painting "word pictures."

PICTURES ON A THEME

Some movement and word "pictures" can be based on topics or themes suggested by single words or phrases like:

rain	hunting	snow
winter	a fight	robots
volcanoes	a robbery	tides
wind	bubbles	magnets
thunder	flying	magic spells
lightning	vehicles	parades
growing	fires	imprisoned
the sea	cats	copycat
		space ships

Teacher and children talk about the topic, recounting their experiences, their feelings, ideas, and opinions. As they talk, the teacher jots down key words (verbs, nouns, adjectives, and adverbs) used by the children, adding others, as well. If winter is the topic, words collected by the teacher might include:

snow swirls	wind blows	flutter
white flakes	wind flutters	descent
snow whirls	wind howls	white
fall	breeze	whistle
melt	cold	sweep
freeze	dance	

The teacher accepts all the words the children suggest, even though the list may be long. Later, a few words are selected from the list (and others added if desired) for movement exploration and improvisation. For example:

Snow: swirl, flutter, freeze
Wind: race, swirl, collapse

Once the children have improvised their own dances, they are ready to write original compositions describing what they imagined or what they may remember from a personal experience. They now fall back on all words which they and their classmates used earlier.

Some children respond well to lessons planned around a theme; others want additional guidance or stimulus to help them imagine a story. A picture, an artifact, a musical recording or tape will give the group more ideas for writing. Words that captured the imagination of the children during the original discussion or movement will now surface, especially if the long list is left on the blackboard. Others that failed to inspire the children will be ignored. The teacher should not force the children to use all the words.

PICTURES FROM STORIES AND POEMS

Movement and word pictures can also be structured from stories and poems that the group reads together from published sources. As before, teacher and children discuss the topic while the teacher records key words suggested by the children, perhaps adding a few more. Some of the words are gathered from the selection, supplemented by others if necessary. (Chapter 2 gives detailed information on selecting words for movement.) Again more words than are used in movement are collected and left on the board for creative writing sessions.

An excellent example of the way writing can be developed from literature is provided by the work done by a fifth–sixth grade group with the poem "The Wind Has Wings," already mentioned in chapters 1 and 2. The children and their teacher generated the following word list (describing *wind* and *bird of prey*) after they had heard and discussed the poem:

strong	soaring
evil	dark
harsh	frightening
cold	claw
cutting	tear
relentless	twist
never-ceasing	run
bird of prey	leap
eagle	

As can be seen in the poem that follows and those appearing in chapter 1, many words on this list surfaced in the children's writing.

Sometimes the wind is bitter.
It stomps and leaps around our house.
And howls through the cracks at the door.
It tears and rips at the trees
So the leaves whirl to the ground.

Sometimes the wind is kind.
It whistles past the door
(and sings through the window.)
It waves at the flowers
So they sway and twist, bending a little.
—Allyson, 6th Grade

SUMMARY

When movement is used as a response to language and literature, all aspects of language are brought to bear on the lesson, ensuring thereby that language development will be fostered. Attentive listening is emphasized, word meaning highlighted. The children have many opportunities to read aloud and deepen comprehension.

Movement lessons also lead into creative drama and writing. Teachers will be more successful in relating expressive movement to language arts with carefully planned questions and lessons emphasizing the words around which movement lessons are designed. Using the methods suggested in this chapter, the teacher can use movement to have a significant effect on the language arts.

BIBLIOGRAPHY ON
LANGUAGE ARTS ACTIVITIES
THAT UTILIZE MOVEMENT

Boorman, Joyce. *Dance and Language Experience with Children*. Don Mills, Ontario: Longmans, 1973.

Chenfield, Mimi Brodsky. *Teaching Language Arts Creatively*. New York: Harcourt Brace Jovanovich, 1978.

Hennings, Dorothy Grant. *Communication in Action*. New York: Rand McNally, 1978.

Logan, William M., & Logan, Virgil G. *A Dynamic Approach to the Language Arts*. Toronto: McGraw-Hill, 1967.

Moffett, James. *Teaching the Universe of Discourse*. Boston: Houghton Mifflin, 1968.

Moffett, James. *The Student-Centered Language Arts Curriculum, K–13*. Boston: Houghton Mifflin, 1968.

Van Allen, Roach. *Language Experiences in Communication*. Boston: Houghton Mifflin, 1976.

II

MODEL LESSONS

5

Explorations

The lessons in this chapter are designed for groups exploring movement for the first time. Teachers and children may use each lesson to get acquainted with basic movement concepts: for instance, how to move safely in a large space when twenty or more children are moving in the same area. At the same time, these introductory lessons call for a response to literature and language that involves children in listening, speaking, and reading. Teachers will also find many of the explorations useful in breaking down resistance to expressive movement sometimes found among children in the upper grades (particularly boys).

Teachers beginning to use movement with an inexperienced group must learn to be sensitive to the children's needs. Although young children in the early grades are always eager to take part in movement lessons, they often need help exploring ways to move their bodies. Older boys and girls in grades five to eight are often capable of performing many basic exploratory movements, but they can be very self-conscious in the presence of peers. Lessons in this chapter are meant to overcome both difficulties.

POINTS TO KEEP IN MIND

Before embarking on expressive movement in the classroom, there are some important points every teacher should keep in mind and follow through on.

Encouraging Inventiveness

Whatever the level of movement, genuine inventiveness should be encouraged in all lessons. Certain kinds of teacher behavior will help establish a climate that encourages creativity.

First, teachers must consciously seek divergent answers by assigning tasks that can be done in a number of ways. For example:

> Invent your own bridge with two of you working together.
> Find two ways to make a bridge alone.

Second, teachers must always observe pupils carefully during lessons, noting the way the boys and girls perform explorations, looking for children who experiment with an idea more creatively or competently, and asking these children to show the class what they did. Positive feedback and divergent solutions are thus emphasized.

Using Space Safely

Children without movement experience often stand in tight clumps or form circles. They don't leave enough space around themselves for safety. Therefore, throughout all movement lessons it is important to stress safe use of space. Frequent reminders and considerable practice will help the class learn to compensate for the traffic moving around them while concentrating on their own pathways. A good way to start every lesson is to say something like, "Find your own space." The same message should be repeated whenever children leave large, empty spots on the floor or crowd too closely (see figure 7).

Making the Most of Jumps

Special attention should be paid to jumping, leaping, and turning, because all must be executed safely and because they add excitement to explorations and improvisations (see figure 8).

Jumps may be broken down and taught in three parts—the takeoff, body shape in flight, and the landing—each of which is broken down further. The takeoff is made from the right, left, or both feet with varying degrees of thrust. The stronger the thrust from the floor, the more powerful the jump. Jumps from both feet take the body high into the air, while leaps from one foot allow the body to gain length as well as height. Body shape in the air may be

Figure 7. It is important to stress safe use of space. Frequent reminders and considerable practice help the class learn to compensate for traffic.

wide or thin, symmetrical or asymmetrical, as arms and legs gesture or the body twists or turns completely before landing. Landings, which may take place onto one or two feet, become resilient enough to absorb jarring when knees are either light and bouncy or deeply bent. Children can become aware of jumps and perform them more effectively if the teacher allows sufficient practice in all three phases.

Helping Children Remember Pathways

Children often have trouble remembering the paths they followed while moving from one place to another. Since remembering pathways can be important in improvisation, it is wise to give children ample practice retracing paths they have already covered. Scatter some children around the floor as guideposts for those walking, skipping, or running. Children moving about the room will be

Figure 8. Special attention should be paid to jumping, leaping, and turning, because all must be executed with care.

able to use classmates who are standing still as clues for their next movements.

Establishing a Signal for Silence

It is important to establish some kind of signal for silence very early in the lessons. An effective one is a light tap on a tambourine. Tell the children to walk anywhere in the class but be ready to "freeze" (stand absolutely still) when they hear the tambourine (or drum or whistle). If the teacher makes a game of this—for instance, by asking the children to "freeze" in a shape like a witch, a giant, a puppet—the group will listen carefully, enjoy themselves, and obey instantaneously.

When they are moving, the children can walk, skip, bounce, run, or travel in any other way. Stop signals should be given at irregular intervals to test their concentration. The signals can vary; the teacher may clap hands, hit a percussion instrument, or tell the group to be quiet. The softer the sound the greater the test for listening as the children move more lightly to hear the stop sound.

EXPLORATORY GAMES

When working with children who seem self-conscious, it is wise to introduce them to expressive movement through games. Emphasis on play quickly involves even the most reluctant. Here are some activities that will serve this purpose.

1. We are going to walk in different directions. Can you think of three ways to walk (jump, run, skip, hop) forward (backward, sideways)?
2. Invent your own way of walking (running, skipping) while you lead with elbows (knees, one of your ears, your chin, etc.).
3. When I give you a signal, walk in any direction in a straight line. Turn sharply in any direction on the bang of the tambourine (or drum). Go in a different direction each time you hear the tambourine or drum. (Same lesson can be developed around other locomotions.)
4. Walk (run, hop, skip) in a path of your own invention, counting as you go. Turn sharply after two (four, six, eight, or some other number) steps.
5. How many ways can you find for getting from one place to another without using your feet?
6. Devise your own pathway using a curved, twisted, or straight path. When you retrace your steps, add something like a jump, leap, or roll.
7. Find your own way of walking so that you are stretched as high as possible while moving on the balls of your feet. As you walk, fall slowly down to your knees. Then rise slowly so that you are stretched as high as possible. Now try the same movement while jumping (hopping, twisting, turning, etc.).
8. Run and jump, sometimes taking off with one foot, sometimes with two (see figure 9).
9. Run and show two different kinds of jumps. Jump for height and then for length.

Figure 9. This is a run and jump starting on one foot and landing on the other.

10. Work with a partner. "A" makes a very small shape for "B" to jump over. "A" tells "B" how heavy his landing was. Exchange places.
11. Run and jump making yourself as wide (thin) as possible in the air (see figure 10).
12. Perform the same run and jump, but this time make your feet kick before you land.
13. Run and do a turning jump.
14. Sit on the floor. Take your feet and hands off the floor. Push yourself into a spin with your hands. Can you spin without a push? Do the same standing.
15. Take a starting position close to the floor with plenty of "give" in both knees. As you spin, rise higher. Let your arms lead you upward (see figure 11).
16. Find a partner. Face him or her and hold hands. Now spin. Gather speed. Then slow down. Find another way to spin with your partner.

17. Make a big shape with your whole body and then change the shape to a small one like the big one. Make your shape round (crooked, twisted, straight) (see figure 12).

18. Use a hoop, rope, scarf, or paper to form a shape. Make your body into a similar shape.

19. Balance your body so that it touches the ground in two (three, four, five) places. Can you try the same idea using one foot (one arm, one knee, your head, etc.)?

20. Walk until I bang my tambourine (or drum). Then freeze into a _____ (suggest monsters, puppets, geometric figures, or other shapes; with older children abstract terms like poverty, wretchedness, hatred, anger are also excellent choices).

Figure 10. A primary-grade boy does a run and jump, making himself as thin as possible in the air.

Figure 11. The group spins and lets arms lead them upward.

21. Move any way you like as slowly as possible. When you hear the signal, perform the same motion as fast as possible.

22. You are a toy that is wound up. Move mechanically, first fast, slowing down gradually to a stop. Perform the same action smoothly.

23. Work in pairs. One "shadows" the other, moving in exactly the same way as the first person. As the two of you move around the room, change your walk so that you run, walk, creep, or roll, moving slow and then fast. Try the same actions moving mechanically and then smoothly, lightly and then heavily.

24. I (the teacher) am going to be the "cat." You will be the "mice." Creep from the sides of the wall toward me. When I bang my tambourine (or drum), dash back to the walls.

25. Divide into two groups. We are going to play "tug of war" with an imaginary rope. Pull on the "rope" with as much tension as you can manage. Hold your body so that it shows tension all over. Where would you hold your hands (feet, head)?

26. On the bang of the tambourine (or drum) grab some part of your body and collapse suddenly as if you were hit. Repeat the same action, this time sinking slowly. (As the children repeat the collapse ask them to vary the place of impact.)

27. I am going to work out a rhythm pattern on a tambourine. Reproduce the pattern together after I am done. (The teacher may prefer to use hands and feet slapping, clapping, and stamping. The pattern should contrast force, speed and rhythm.)

28. Working with a partner, try to mirror exactly what your partner does. The leader should try pushing, pulling, bending, stretching, twisting, swinging, rising and falling, walking, rolling, running, hopping and jumping. Look at the

Figure 12. Partners make a twisted shape.

exact position of your partner's feet, head, fingers. Move very slowly and duplicate the action exactly.

29. Working in a group, pass around a fast or slow movement using different parts of the body. As the action moves from person to person, vary the movement with pushes, pulls, bends, stretches, twists, swings or falls.

30. Two children work together. Build an object with your bodies. After you are done, we will guess what you have done or made. (Some possible objects: a house; a machine with synchronized moving parts; a box; a factory assembly line; an ornate clock with figures moving around it. See chapter 3 for a verbal obbligato devised by a group who "made" a machine.)

EXPLORATIONS IN RESPONSE TO LITERATURE

Like the games described above, the explorations in this section will help children get acquainted with basic movement concepts without improvising a dance. Teachers can view all the lessons that follow as unfinished and as first explorations. When children are further acquainted with expressive movement, all of these explorations can be further developed so that they become improvisations. At that point, either teacher or children may take the lead in creating an improvised dance around a sequence.

Exploration 1: Freeze!

An interesting way to introduce stopping and listening is to show the children a book like *Laughing Camera for Children*, by Hanns Reich (New York: Hill and Wang, 1971). Afterwards, the children walk around the room in any direction until the teacher "takes a picture" of them by tapping a tambourine. The children then "freeze" in a shape as if a photograph was taken of them.

The teacher will help the children freeze in a variety of shapes by posing problems like:

Find two ways to make a picture so that three points of your body touch the ground.

Find three ways to freeze close to the ground.

Freeze in a shape that is tall and thin.

Make a very big shape.

It is important to tap the tambourine in an *irregular* pattern, to ensure that children listen carefully.

Some other books that lend themselves to freezing and making shapes are:

Udry, Janice May. *The Moon Jumpers*. New York: Harper & Row, 1959.
Zemach, Harve. *The Judge*. New York: Farrar, Straus & Giroux, 1969.

Older children will enjoy responding to:

Asch, Frank. *Elvira Everything*. New York: Harper & Row, 1970.
Raskin, Ellen. *Nothing Ever Happens on My Block*. New York: Atheneum, 1966.

Exploration 2: Traffic

To set the stage for "traffic," Dorothy Baruch's poem "Stop—Go" may be used:

Stop — Go

Automobiles in a row
Wait to go
While the signal says STOP.

Bells ring
Tingaling
Red light's gone!
Green light's on!
Horns blow!
And the row starts to GO.
—Dorothy Baruch

A provocative way to introduce spacing, this game allows children to explore the ways in which different kinds of road traffic move. In the exploration, the teacher becomes the policeman, directing traffic and telling which vehicles stop or go. The poem, with its visual and auditory imagery for various kinds of signals, and its rhythms suggesting various rates of motion (or immobility), creates interest. The teacher can use the occasion to teach the concept *vehicle* as one that encompasses all the cars, trucks, and other vehicles to be involved in the lesson.

After hearing and discussing the poem, the group decide how the vehicles will move. Some possibilities could be:

Taxis—run
Automobiles—walk as fast as possible
Trucks—go on all fours (hands and feet)
Trolley cars—skip in pairs

The children then practice moving, listening (or watching) carefully for signals from the teacher, who is acting as policeman. (To relate this lesson to reading, the teacher could use lettered signs—STOP, GO, TURN, and others—as cues.) The teacher reminds the children to space themselves around the room, at the same time keeping adequate control and speed. The children will explore their movements more fully if the teacher tells them to perform tasks like:

Everyone is a car, walking very fast.
Try walking with very big steps.
Now see if you can walk fast while you take quick, little steps.

Everyone is a taxi, running very fast.
As you run, be careful.
Don't bump into anyone.

You can now all be trolley cars.
Try holding hands and skipping side by side.
Try skipping one behind the other, next to each other.

Now select your own vehicle. Make sure you pay attention to my signals.

Another poem children enjoy with this exploration is "I'm the Police Cop Man, I Am" by Margaret Morrison, in *The Sound of*

Poetry, compiled by Mary Austen (Boston: Allyn & Bacon, 1965).

Exploration 3: Popcorn

This exploration, which involves a creative response to a popular picture book, features oral language and listening as well as the physical act of jumping.

The group begin the lesson by listening to *The Popcorn Book*, by Tomie de Paola (New York: Scholastic, 1978), and respond afterwards by "becoming" the popcorn. On a signal, the boys and girls "pop" (jump) as they "change" from kernels to popcorn.

To help the class explore the possibilities, the teacher may give instructions like:

Curl up tightly. With both your feet bent deeply, jump straight up into the air.

Try another starting position. Jump straight up.

Bend low and on a signal jump from one foot to another. Jump forward. Now jump sideways.

The exploration will be more interesting if the teacher uses several signals (perhaps a combination of voice, tambourine, and bell). Each child would then listen for a different signal, and children would jump up at different times. The lesson will also gain interest if sounds suggesting popcorn popping are produced by a choral group or by individual children stationed on one side of the room.

Exploration 4: Rosie's Walk

Rosie's Walk, by Pat Hutchins (New York: Macmillan, 1968) is a delightful story about a hen who is followed by a fox as she goes for a walk through the farmyard. The lesson developed around it has several purposes. The children become acquainted with an amusing tale. The teacher helps children remember pathways they have learned, using the story as a vehicle. In addition, the lesson provides an excellent way to introduce children to the meanings of common function words in the English language (words like *over*, *under*, *through*). These words (frequently called Dolch words among reading teachers) are usually included in early reading programs as begin-

Figure 13. A page from *Rosie's Walk* by Pat Hutchins (New York: Collier Books, 1971). Reprinted with permission of Macmillan Publishing Co., Inc., and The Bodley Head, Ltd., London. Copyright © 1968 by Patricia Hutchins.

ning sight words. Frequently, first-graders do not understand their meanings. Children can easily learn the definitions of the words by associating them with body movements. By holding up cards with the function words written on them, the teacher may help the class learn to read basic sight words. Adding action words—like *hop*, *skip*, *walk*, *march*, *slide*, *tiptoe*—will add variety to the movement and additional practice in reading.

First, the teacher reads the story to the group, showing them the pictures. The pictures suggest *how* the fox and hen move. The text provides the cues that tell *where* the body moves. With the fox close at her heels, Rosie travels

Across the yard	Past the mill
Around the pond	Through the fence
Over the haystack	Under the beehives

Next, the children take a partner and play follow-the-leader. Skipping, walking, or combining the two actions, they move around the room, changing leaders frequently. The teacher holds up cards and reminds the group to keep adequate space around each child.

Some children now become "obstacles" of different shapes and sizes—the yard, the pond, the haystack, the mill, the fence, the beehive. Questions like the following will help the children explore the possibilities:

Can you make a low shape close to the ground so that someone could step *over* you?

Can you make a high shape so that someone could go *under* you?

It is important to observe the children's variations, allowing time for demonstration and further practice.

Now, the teacher invites the children to think of two different ways of getting across and around some objects of similar size, and the class divides into groups of two. One person becomes an obstacle, one becomes Rosie. The "obstacles" space themselves over the floor in high or low positions, and a few hoops and other objects are scattered around the floor as well. From their different starting positions the "Rosies" begin their journeys at a signal from the teacher, who then proceeds to give a series of instructions for dealing with obstacles (over, under, through, around, . . .). Each Rosie creates a pathway that goes over, around, under, through, and across a series of obstacles.

Exploration 5: Messages

Children enjoy this exploration because they can send messages through rhythmical body movement and speech. Teachers find it valuable because listening and sequencing are highlighted as responses to a book of high interest to boys and girls.

Introduce the exploration by reading John Stewig's book, *Sending Messages* (Boston: Houghton Mifflin, 1978). After talking about the many ways messages can be transmitted (written words, spoken words, repeated sounds, concrete symbols, body language), the children divide into two groups. One group "sends," by tapping fingers, pounding feet, clicking fingernails, snapping fingers, or using any other kinds of body movement or words to make up a rhythmical pattern. The other group "receives," and members answer with their own messages. The teacher will help the children explore the rhythmical patterns by demonstrating several and asking the group to respond.

The children will be more inventive about body movement and sounds they use if the teacher asks questions like:

Do you want to make your message emphatic? Stamp your foot very hard or jump straight up, landing hard. Slap your neighbor's or your own hand. Hit the floor or wall with your open hand. Make a large noise with your voice.

Try a quiet sound, tapping the floor with your fingers or your foot. Make a quiet sound with your voice.

Try a different rhythm.

Make up a verbal obbligato (see "Verbal Sounds," chapter 3). Take any words (two or three) and arrange them in a repetitive rhythmical pattern. Also make a pattern of sounds with your body. Put them all together and send your message.

Exploration 6: Machines

Homer Price, by Robert McCloskey (New York: Viking, 1943) is a story that has amused readers for generations. Its tongue-in-cheek hyperbole is epitomized in the doughnut machine episode.

Homer devises a "wonderful doughnut machine," which is delightfully illustrated in the book. While he is taking care of his uncle's shop, he makes a batch of dough in the wonderful new machine with the help of a bum, a mysterious rich lady, and her chauffeur. Long after the lady and her chauffeur have gone off into the night, the machine cranks out the doughnuts endlessly. The exploratory lesson that follows allows the children to capture something of the exaggeration and the mechanical movement of the machine. This is an excellent introductory exploration for older children who have never tried expressive movement before, often drawing in even the most reluctant.

The teacher can encourage the children to make their own doughnut "machines," in a variety of ways, with instructions like:

Figure 14. A page from *Homer Price* by Robert McCloskey (Scholastic Book Services edition). Copyright © 1943, © renewed 1971 by Robert McCloskey. Reprinted by permission of Viking Penguin Inc.

Make a hole with both hands.

Make a hole with one hand.

Now do the same thing with your whole body.

Working with a partner, make a hole between you.

One partner make a bridge. The other rolls under it.

Invent a machine in which one of you moves in one direction and the other moves in a different one. Create a sound effect that fits your machine.

Help the children move with comments like:

Move in different directions on two feet, on all fours, while standing in one place. Your machine moves very jerkily up and down and/or from side to side.

One of you may wind up the other, who starts to move. The first now copies the second, mirror image. After a while the two of you reverse positions.

Now four of you make a machine. At intervals a doughnut can roll out of your machine. Make appropriate sound effects as your doughnut rolls out.

If ideas do not flow easily, the children can mime simple machines and then vary the speed, size, and direction. Some possibilities are a see-saw, piston machine, sewing machine, a machine with a conveyor belt. In addition, inspiration might be found in the following books, in which children invent or use "Rube Goldberg" machines:

Raskin, Ellen. *Franklin Stein*. New York: Atheneum, 1972.
Williams, Jay, & Abrashkin, Raymond. *Danny Dunn and the Smalli-fying Machine*. New York: McGraw-Hill, 1969.
Williams, Jay, & Abrashkin, Raymond. *Danny Dunn and the Homework Machine*. New York: McGraw-Hill, 1958.

Exploration 7: Shadowing

This lesson is effective as an introductory activity for older children and as a way to explore the concrete meaning of the poem "Shadows." Begin by sharing the poem with your group.

Shadows

Chunks at night
Melt
In the morning sun.
One lonely one
Grows legs
And follows me
To school.
    —Patricia Hubbell

After the poem has been read, ask the children to try shadowing each other exactly. They will be more inventive about the ways they shadow or mirror each other if the teacher poses problems like:

Find a partner.

Face each other. One is the leader. The other moves exactly the same as the first. You *must* move *very* slowly because it is very hard to follow the actions of someone who is moving quickly.

Try tracing geometric shapes with your arms.

Include your legs, your whole body. Try dancing, prancing, slowing.

Pretend one of you is eating. The other is the person's shadow.

Suddenly the shadow is transformed into a real person. There are two of you sitting in a restaurant eating dinner. What happens?

You are done. One leaves the restaurant and the second follows.

Suddenly you are transformed. One of you is a boy going to school. The other is a shadow. Move very slowly as if you were moving in slow motion. Take exaggerated steps. Move sideways, forward. Involve your whole body in your movement.

Exploration 8: Bundles

These lines from the poem "Bundles," by John Farrar, suggest all sorts of shapes.

> A bundle is a funny thing,
> It always sets me wondering:
> For whether it is thin or wide
> You never know just what's inside.
> —John Farrar

The children explore some of the possibilities in the lesson that follows. Here are a number of directions they might be given.

Make the shape of a bundle or a parcel with your hands. Make a little one. Now make a great big one.

Can you make the shape of a parcel with your whole body?

What is the shape of the string that ties your bundle?

Show me a knot in the string.

Decide what you would like to have in a parcel; then make the shape the parcel might have. (After the children have made their shapes, the teacher may ask what is in them.)

Make a parcel shape with a friend.

Make your parcel flat, high, round, twisted, thin, wide.

BIBLIOGRAPHY ON EXPLORATIONS AND THEATER GAMES

Barnfield, Gabriel. *Creative Drama in Schools*. New York: Hart Publishing, 1968.

Boorman, Joyce. *Creative Dance in the Primary Grades*. Don Mills, Ontario: Longmans, 1971.

Boorman, Joyce. *Creative Dance in Grades 4 to 6*. Don Mills, Ontario: Longmans, 1971.

Dimondstein, Geraldine. *Exploring the Arts with Children*. New York: Macmillan, 1974.

Elkind, Sam. *Improvisation Handbook*. Chicago: Scott, Foresman, 1975.

Goodridge, Janet. *Drama in the Primary School*. London: Heinemann, 1971.

Learmouth, John, & Whitaker, Keith. *Movement in Practice*. Boston: Plays, Inc., 1977.

Ranger, Paul. *Experiments in Drama*. London: University of London Press, 1970.

Russell, Joan. *Creative Dance in the Primary School*. London: MacDonald and Evans, 1965.

Spolin, Viola. *Improvisation in the Theater*. Evanston, Ill.: Northwestern University, 1973.

Way, Brian. *Development Through Drama*. London: Longmans, 1973.

6

Improvisations:
The Primary Years

Once the group has had a little practice exploring what their bodies can do, they are ready for an important step forward—improvising their own dances. Important learning beyond movement takes place at the level of exploration, as well as in improvisation. Both exploratory and improvisational expressive movement provide young children with easy access to understanding through concrete experience, literally enabling them to *experience* what a word means, what it is like to be in someone else's shoes, what a strange setting in a story is like, what a rhythmic pattern feels like. Both levels of movement are also valuable as vehicles for communicating feelings: for example, the joy of playing with the teacher, or the fears and excitement that well up on meeting a "monster." In short, expressive movement allows children to learn as whole human beings.

Only at the level of improvisation, however, is the children's creative potential tapped. In each lesson that follows the teacher first helps the children explore the possibilities for movement during explorations and then lets them improvise their own combinations or sequences. Improvisations are, therefore, ways in which boys and girls express what they personally think and feel about a selection.

Frequently these interpretations can alert the teacher to the children's understanding of the selection, indicating clearly whether or not they were able to grasp the main idea, the meanings of words, the plot, characters, or setting. In order to establish how well the class understands the material, teachers should watch improvisations carefully, while asking themselves these questions:

88

- Are the children interpreting vocabulary correctly?
- Do they understand the main idea?
- Do they understand the setting, plot, and characters of the story?
- Are they responding to the rhythm with reasonable sensitivity?
- Are they capturing the mood of the selection?

Every point need not be considered for every improvisation.

Each lesson in this chapter and in chapter 7 is built either around a poem or around a specific theme which is presented and discussed at the beginning, before the movement work is outlined. The movement work itself starts with explorations, which are used to introduce children to movement concepts needed for the lesson. The second section of each lesson deals with improvisations, when children invent their own dances. A third section, entitled "Extending the Lesson," is intended as a guide for teachers who wish to take advantage of the interest and excitement invariably engendered by movement for further related work in the language arts.

LESSON 1: "PETER WHITE"

In this lesson, young children become acquainted with a nursery rhyme not commonly included in Mother Goose collections.

Peter White[1]

Peter White
Will ne'er go right.
Would you know the reason why?

He follows his nose
Wherever he goes
And that stands all awry.

—Anon.

Children always enjoy hearing Mother Goose rhymes. They are delighted with the rhythm, the strange words, the pleasure of a

---

[1]Iona & Peter Opie, *A Family Book of Nursery Rhymes* (New York: Oxford University Press, 1964).

shared moment spent with an adult. They do not always grasp—nor do they need to—the full meaning of these poems, many of which have archaic or uncommon words (and arcane historical reference at times). But a response through movement can help them understand the literal meaning of the entire poem or a few words in it.

Through movement, the lines "Peter White / Will ne'er go right" and "He follows his nose / Wherever he goes" are given a concrete reference, as is the difficult word *awry*. In follow-up work, vocabulary and concept development are underlined as children discover other shapes that are *straight* and *crooked*, *symmetrical* and *asymmetrical*. A bibliography of books that offer ideas for expanding the concepts is included under "Extending the Lesson."

The exploratory movement introduces the class to upside-down shapes and zigzag pathways brought about by sudden changes in direction as the children walk. An occasional child may hesitate when asked to "turn your nose" during explorations. It is important to make sure that children who seem bewildered understand the meaning of the directions. To ensure that the pupils relate words and movement, the exploratory phase of the lesson may need to be repeated several times.

Explorations

After the children hear the rhyme, the teacher asks the group which way their noses are pointing, with questions like:

> Where else could you point your noses—forward, down, up toward different sides?

The teacher taps a drum, and the children, who are seated, quickly respond by pointing their noses (turning their heads) in different directions. After they swing just their heads a few times, the children find adequate spaces for themselves where they next shift their whole bodies in new directions when the drum bangs. Then, on a signal from the teacher the children walk about briskly in a zigzag pathway, which they invent themselves, turning sharp corners (pointing their noses and bodies in directions which they choose) when the teacher hits the tambourine.

The last line, "and that stands all awry," which suggests a final upside-down or crooked position, will require some experimentation. Upside-down positions can mean many things to children, including head between knees, weight on hands, headstands, weight on shoulders with feet in the air, and a host of semi-upside-down positions, frequently with twists and turns added. The children will be more inventive if the teacher asks questions like:

> Can you find an upside-down position with your feet the highest part of you?
>
> Can you twist your legs from that position?
>
> Can you make your elbows the highest part of you?
>
> Find two different crooked shapes.

Improvisation

Children combine a zigzag pathway they have already invented with their favorite crooked and/or upside-down shape. First they zigzag, then they stop and "stand awry." Tambourine or drum can be an accompaniment. Although children generally respond to this activity enthusiastically, the teacher will need to remind the class to use pathways and shapes they tried during the explorations.

Extending the Lesson

Building on the children's understanding of *awry*, the teacher can extend their vocabulary further, developing the concepts *symmetrical* and *asymmetrical* with the following questions and activities:

> Can you make a shape which is awry?
>
> Is your shape crooked or straight? (Straight should be defined as *balanced*.)
>
> Make another shape that is crooked or straight.
>
> Another word for *straight* or *balanced* is *symmetrical*. Another word for *crooked* is *asymmetrical*. Make a symmetrical shape with your body. Make an asymmetrical shape with your body.

The following books will also help children understand the meaning of *symmetrical* and *asymmetrical*:

Carle, Eric. *My Very First Book of Shapes*. New York: Crowell, 1974.
Walter, Marion. *Make a Bigger Puddle: Made a Smaller Worm*. London: Deutsch, 1971.
Hoban, Tana. *Shapes and Things*. New York: Macmillan, 1970.
Riess, John. *Shapes*. London: Hamilton Hamish, 1973.

LESSON 2: "SEESAW"

Rhythm is as natural to us as the steady beat of a heart. Whether steady and monotonous or wildly erratic, rhythm sets the pace that times our lives in many ways. The ticking of a clock may tell us when to wake up. The rhythm of the tides tells fishermen when to set sail. The rhythm of the seasons tells farmers when to plant. Thus rhythm affects all of us deeply.

Evelyn Beyer's poem communicates sounds and feelings as it represents a seesaw swinging rhythmically up and down.

Seesaw

Up and down,
Up and down,
Seesaws pop
Up,
Seesaws drop
Down.
The down is a bump,
The up is a jump.
Seesaw,
Seesaw, UP!
　　　　　—Evelyn Beyer

Like the motion of the seesaw, the poem is full of surprises. The surprises offer amusing opportunities for a game and an improvisation that invariably delight boys and girls and that later may be turned to advantage in work with vocabulary and concepts.

Figure 15. The teacher becomes the children's collective partner during explorations of "Seesaw."

Explorations

The children crouch on the floor with ample space around them. They jump as high as they can, flinging their arms high above their heads. This action is repeated several times while the teacher sets a rhythm, beating a percussion instrument (perhaps a tambourine).

With the children facing her, the teacher now becomes their collective partner. As she goes up, the children go down, and vice versa. (See figure 15.) When the children are responding well, the teacher may vary the movement by:

Moving quickly with or without surprise changes in speed

Moving and stopping on the way up or down

Moving with the children at the same time and in the same direction

Improvisation

The children next choose partners. The twosomes hold hands, leaning away from each other or simply standing opposite each other. One goes up as the other goes down. Alternatively, the children can choose to hit their fists on the floor for "the down is a bump" and spring off the floor abruptly, for "the up is a jump." They should be encouraged to improvise their own action.

The poem makes an excellent accompaniment for the improvisation. The whole class may recite it, emphatically and with a lively tempo, as they improvise. Or half the group may recite the poem while the other half invent their movement sequence. A tambourine or drum will also serve very well to establish effective rhythmic accompaniment.

The same movement game may be used with the poem "The Swing" in *Hello and Goodbye*, by Mary Ann Hoberman (Boston: Little, Brown, 1959).

Extending the Lesson

The teacher can extend the children's comprehension of opposites by pointing out that *up* and *down* are opposites and then asking them to make their bodies into:

Big and little shapes
Round and flat shapes
Fat and thin shapes
Crooked and straight shapes
High and low shapes

and to move:

Fast and slow
Twisting and turning
Pushing and pulling

The concept of opposites may be explored further through the following books:

Hoban, Tana. *Push, Pull, Empty, Full*. New York: Macmillan, 1972.
Hoban, Tana. *Over, Under and Through*. New York: Macmillan, 1973.
Spier, Peter. *Fast-Slow; High-Low*. New York: Doubleday, 1972.

LESSON 3: RAIN

A perfect time to undertake this lesson is a rainy day when children cannot go outdoors for exercise. The improvisation in which they create their own "rain happening," gives children an opportunity for much activity and sets the stage for an interesting experience in writing. Throughout the lesson, listening carefully is stressed.

The teacher starts with a request for words that describe rain falling. A typical class will offer some of the following:

plip-plop	lightning
pitter-patter	splash
sprinkling	crash
hailing	crackle
thundering	boom-bang

Explorations

The children next explore words like *plip-plop* or *pitter-patter*. The teacher asks for actions such as these:

While you sit on the floor, tap the floor lightly and slowly with your toes.

While sitting on the floor, use your fingers to make a sound like "pitter-patter."

Pick up the same rhythm with your feet.

Move around the floor while you continue the same pattern of sounds. Walk some of the time; run some of the time.

Try running in a straight or curved line.

Half of you sit around the room making a sound with your hands—you might clap or tap the floor with your fingernails. The other half run quickly around the seated people and then back to your starting position.

Now the class explores more forceful movements, suggested by words like *thunder, crash, crackle, boom, bang.* Actions such as the following could be requested:

Run forcefully on the spot, trying to make a lot of sound.

Stride all over the floor with very large strong steps.

Try leaping and jumping as you walk.

Alternate "thudding" on the spot with strong, bouncing leaps while traveling.

Punch with both hands, one after the other, at an imaginary target above your head.

The "rain happening" will be more successful and the children will synthesize their ideas better if they can use sound effects. Here are some directions they can be given for making sound effects with drums, tambourines, their hands, or feet.

Tap the surface of your drum or tambourine with your fingernails.

Scrape the surface of your instrument.

Tap the wooden frame with a drumstick.

Tap the floor with your fingernails.

Clap your hands continuously.

Drum the floor with your feet while sitting (or standing).

Hammer the floor with your fists.

Improvisation

After the children have explored many movements and tried to make a variety of sounds, they are ready for their own "rain happening." Each one works with a partner. The teacher can help the children structure their improvisations by suggesting that they select two ways of moving lightly and two ways of moving with force. The improvisations will require practice, and time should be allowed for it.

Extending the Lesson

When the children have listed words, explored sound effects, and improvised a dance, they will be ready to write effectively. They have had an exhilarating experience, and they have had ample time to play with some ideas as they improvised a dance. Before them on the blackboard is a list of vivid words they can use in their writing.

The kind of writing that can result is demonstrated by the following compositions produced by a group of second-grade children after a movement improvisation about rain:

> First the clouds move in. Then it gets cold out. Then it starts
> sprinkling. Then it gets harder and harder and then sometimes it
> hails. And thunder and lightning. Smash, crack, crash, boom, bang,
> bam, pitter, patter, patter, splash.
>
> —Stacey, 2nd Grade
> (See figure 16)

> Pitter, Patter. The rain sprinkled on the umbrellas. The people ran
> home where it was warm.
>
> —Carolyn, 2nd Grade

> First the rain falls softly. Plitter-Platter. Plip-plop. Down the street it

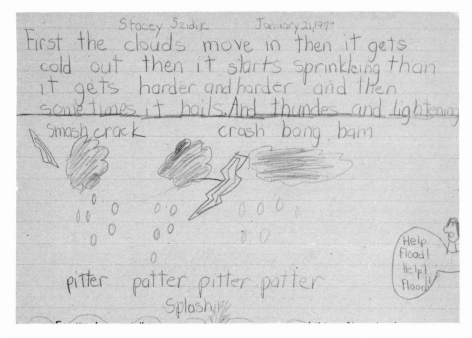

Stacey Szidik   January 21, 1977

First the clouds move in then it gets
cold out then it starts sprinkleing than
it gets harder and harder and then
sometimes it hails. And thundes and lightening
smash crack   crash bang bam

pitter patter pitter patter
Splash

Help
flood!
Help!
flood!

Figure 16. A composition and drawing done by a second-grade child after developing an improvisation that used *rain* as a stimulus.

> runs. Then the rain rains More . . . More . . . and More . . .
> BANG, CRASH, SMASH!
>
> —Kaspar, 2nd Grade

The following books will help the children gain additional ideas about rain storms:

Iwasaki, Chihiro. *Staying Home Alone on a Rainy Day.* New York: McGraw-Hill, 1969.
Shulevitz, Uri. *Rain, Rain, Rivers.* New York: Farrar, Straus & Giroux, 1969.
Zolotow, Charlotte. *The Storm Book.* New York: Harper & Row, 1952.

LESSON 4: "DUCKS' DITTY"

Kenneth Grahame's animal fantasy, *Wind in the Willows*, is a sensitive story reflecting life in England at the turn of the century.

Replete with idyllic descriptions of the peaceful riverbank along which four animals—Ratty, Toad, Mole, and Badger—live, the story is told with measured pace. Perhaps because *Wind in the Willows* takes place in another time and place, the book is not always easily understood or enjoyed by young children today. Fortunately, some of the gap between yesterday and today, there and here, can be spanned for children through movement and drama.

In this lesson, movement improvisation is used to evoke the pastoral setting of a poem from *Wind in the Willows*.

Ducks' Ditty[2]

All along the backwater,
Through the rushes tall,
Ducks are a-dabbling,
Up tails all!

Ducks' tails, Drakes' tails,
Yellow feet a-quiver,
Yellow bills all out of sight
Busy in the river!

Slushy green undergrowth
Where the roach swim—
Here we keep our larder,
Cool and full and dim.

Every one for what he likes!
We like to be
Heads down, tails up,
Dabbling free!

High in the blue above
Swifts whirl and call—
We are down a-dabbling
Up tails all!
                —Kenneth Grahame

A variety of images, only suggested in the poem, are clearly defined in movement improvisation through the use of space. The

---

[2]Kenneth Grahame, *The Wind in the Willows* (New York: Scribner's, 1933).

ducks are severely limited in floor space while the fish, which dart
among the reeds, have a little more room. Only the swifts are allowed the whole floor. During the lesson the children also explore
different upside-down positions. The vocabulary used for the movement improvisation sets the scene for using more vivid language in
effective creative writing, while images created in the dance help the
children develop ideas for artwork like the mural in figure 17.

Explorations

It is best to discuss the poem with the children before exploration or
improvisation is attempted. A good way to start the lesson is to think
of words that might clarify and expand the children's comprehension
of vocabulary used in the poem. The words listed in Table 5 were
discussed by a group of third-grade children.

Figure 17. A mural completed by a group of fourth-graders during lesson
4 on "Ducks' Ditty."

Table 5. Movement Words for "Ducks' Ditty"

Ducks	Roach (fishes)	Reeds	Swifts
waddle	swim	tall	fly
dabble	glide	stretch	whirl
swim	dart	sway	call
dawdle	move quickly	tremble	turn
tip up	up and down	wobble	glide
dive	in and out	slushy	swoop
quiver	turn	drift	wheel
	wriggle		

A short word list was prepared for each category. All of the children explored all of the movements for each of the four lists, with the teacher stressing variation in explorations throughout. A few movements for each category were then worked out for sequences.

Improvisation

After all the movements are explored, an improvised sequence is put together. Reeds do not move at all, but sway in one spot. Ducks move in a very restricted area, roaches over a larger area. Only the swifts may move everywhere (see figures 18 and 19).

Accompaniment

Music is an excellent accompaniment for "Ducks' Ditty"—for instance, a relatively fast waltz with a clear lyrical melody, like "The Waltz" from *Faust* (*Invitation to the Waltz*, by Charles Gounod, Angel Recordings S3622) or "The Wrong Box" (*John Barry Conducts His Greatest Hits*, Columbia, CS9508). Each creature should have his own theme, about two minutes long. The children will need time to listen to the music before they improvise their dance.

Extending the Lesson

After the children have created a dance around the ideas in "Ducks' Ditty," they will have clear ideas about the riverside. They can express their ideas in writing and drawing.

Figure 18. The children whirl and glide, during "Ducks' Ditty."

Figure 19. The children move around the floor as swifts, during "Ducks' Ditty."

LESSON 5: "SONG OF THE TRAIN"

In this poem, David McCord uses a few words to capture the rhythm of a train as it gathers speed and races down the track. The children recapture the beat, movement, and shape of the train, starting slowly and gradually going faster and faster.

Song of the Train

Clickety-clack,
Wheels on the track,
This is the way
They begin the attack:
Click-ety-clack,
Click-ety-clack,
Click-ety-*clack*-ety,
Click-ety
Clack.

Clickety-clack,
Over the crack,
Faster and faster
The song of the track:
Clickety-clack,
Clickety-clack,
Clickety, clackety,
Clackety
Clack.

Riding in front,
Riding in back,
Everyone hears
The song of the track:
Clickety-clack,
Clickety-clack,
Clickety, *clickety*,
Clackety
Clack.

   —David McCord

Exploration

The class is divided into two parts; the first group chants the poem; the second, working in pairs, responds with movement. The explorations themselves are divided into two parts: movement while stationary or on the spot and movement while traveling.

First the children explore *on-the-spot* movement. Clasping each other's hands while standing facing each other, partners move their hands to trace large circles that represent moving wheels. To make the circles as large as possible, the children outline them by pulling up onto their toes for the top of the wheel and brushing the floor for the bottom. The quality of the circles will be improved and the notion of circular pattern in the air extended if the teacher asks each child to:

Make a small circle, then a very large one.

Begin small, and gradually make it larger and larger.

Find another place where you can draw circles . . . at either side, above your heads.

Use an elbow instead of a hand to draw the circle.

The children now join their partners again to work on large, smooth, very round circles (see fig. 20). The two together will become "the train" traveling down the track.

The group now turn to explorations of *traveling*. Because they face each other, the partners generally find it easiest to travel by galloping sideways; but during exploration they should be encouraged to invent their own movement ideas to fit the rhythm of the poem. Suggestions like the following will help them explore some possibilities:

Try galloping as you face each other.

Try skipping while holding hands.

Begin your train ride in the valley and gradually climb the hill.

Make your body move up and down as you travel across the room.

Figure 20. The children join their partners and work on large, smooth, very round circles, during "Song of the Train."

The children will be more inventive about the pathways they follow if the teacher places some markers (hoops, traffic cones, etc.) around the room and suggests ideas like:

> Your train will need to go to as many towns as possible. Each marker is a town.
>
> Do not travel in a straight pathway. Invent one that has at least two turns.

To avoid collisions, the children must look carefully for the spaces they move into. They should also be encouraged to repeat their gallops along the same pathway a second or third time, so as to remember them.

Improvisation

The two parts, *on the spot* and *traveling*, are now put together to create the train, with movement accompanied by recitation of the poem.

The rhythmic pattern for the movement is composed of four counts for outlining four circles (one for each line of the poem) followed by eight counts at twice the speed (two per line in most cases) for traveling. Thus, the first four beats represent the first four lines of the poem. The next eight counts occur during the remaining lines of the stanza. This scheme is repeated for the other stanzas.

The chorus can make the poem and the movement more interesting by varying the speed with which they recite, beginning the first stanza slowly and gradually speeding up so that the second stanza is spoken quite quickly. By the end of the poem, the pace can once more slow down.

Half the class are the chorus, the other half the movement group. The two groups change roles after working through the interpretation. With this procedure, the children observe each other, but are kept actively involved while movement and speech improve together.

Extending the Lesson

Teachers can help the class relate movement experience to language by asking:

What sound does the train make as it moves down the track?
In what way does the poem sound like a train?

The children will understand that the rhythms of the poem and of a train are similar if they make their own train sounds using phrases like "catch-a-teacher" or "patch-his-britches," which catch the rhythm. Arrangements of words with the same syllable count make excellent choral variations for "Song of the Train."

The following selections are also highly rhythmic and lend themselves to various kinds of explorations, including clapping out the rhythm, rhythmic choral interpretation, and vigorous movement.

Baruch, Dorothy. "Merry Go Round." In *Time for Poetry*, edited by M. Arbuthot and S. Root. Glenview, Ill.: Scott, Foresman, 1968.
Brooks, Gwendolyn. "Cynthia in the Snow," from *Bronzeville Boys and Girls*. New York: Harper & Row, 1956.

Farjeon, Eleanor. "Mrs. Peck Pigeon," from *Eleanor Farjeon's Poems for Children*. Philadelphia: Lippincott, 1951.

Hoberman, Mary Ann. "The Swing," from *Hello and Goodby*. Boston: Little, Brown, 1959.

Merriam, Eve. "Onomatopoeia" and "Onomatopoeia II," from *It Doesn't Always Have to Rhyme*. New York: Atheneum, 1966.

LESSON 6: "A LAZY THOUGHT"

With just a few details, "A Lazy Thought" creates two impressionistic pictures that compare the lives of children and adults. Adults lead frenetic lives, rushing around angrily, while children grow in a serene fashion. Even the staccato rhythm of the first part contrasts with the slow pace of the second. The reader must fill in the details with experiences of his own.

A Lazy Thought

There go the grown ups
To the office,
To the store.
Subway rush.
Traffic crush.
Hurry, scurry,
Worry, flurry.

No wonder
Grown ups
Don't grow up
Any more.

It takes a lot
Of slow
To grow.
　　　　　—Eve Merriam

Because children have observed their parents and other adults in action, they generally have little difficulty with the concepts in the poem, which they consider very appealing because children are cast in a positive light while adults are drawn less favorably.

The children also enjoy the quick, confined movement in the first part of the exploration and the broadly different, expanding body movements in the second. The contrasting movements and ideas offer excellent opportunities to talk about the poem and about real life concerns. Children frequently note the differences between the beginning and end of the poem.

Explorations

Before starting the movement lesson, the teacher and children should talk about grownups rushing and bustling about. Questions like the following will encourage children to express their own ideas:

Is your mother (father) ever late? Does she look worried when she (he) is trying to hurry?

What things make you late?

Can you look bad-tempered?

Can you look cross, worried, and hurried as you walk?

The two moods of the poem are expressed through movement in two phases.

During the first verse the children are crowded in a small space. All walk around a well-defined area, twisting and turning to avoid each other, hurrying and then turning suddenly as if remembering something forgotten. As they hurry, the children look worried. No smiling allowed!

During the second verse, there is a sudden change in mood as the children slowly "grow," concentrating on smooth, sustained action. The following suggestions will help the teacher develop a variety of movements in which there is a slow expansion:

Make a tight fist and slowly open your hand until it is fully stretched. Repeat, making the action smoother and slower each time. Try opening your hand in different ways.

Curl up in a small shape. When the tambourine shakes, grow . . . very slowly. (The teacher should shake the tambourine intermittently to make careful listening necessary.)

Tuck your body in so that it is small and so that weight is on both feet. When I have counted to four, you should reach the halfway point. On the next four counts, reach a complete standing position.

Improvisation

The children now put the two parts together. During the first portion they walk quickly in a small area and in twisting, curving pathways while looking cross and worried. During the second section, the children arrange their bodies in small shapes and slowly, carefully grow to full height. As a variation, half of the class can grow while the worried walkers travel around them. After a few minutes the groups change roles.

Extending the Lesson

After discussing their family experiences, the boys and girls will be interested in hearing about other children's encounters with adults. Some books that will help extend and talk about their experiences are:

Ehrlich, Amy. *Zeek Silver Moon.* New York: Dial, 1972.
Buckley, Helen. *Grandfather and I.* New York: Lathrop, 1959.
Scott, Ann Herbert. *Sam.* New York: McGraw-Hill, 1967.
Guilfoile, Elizabeth. *Nobody Listens to Andrew.* New York: Follett, 1957.
Kraus, Robert. *Leo the Late Bloomer.* New York: Windmill, 1971.

LESSON 7: "MRS. CRICKLE-CRACKLE"

This poem develops a character whom children enjoy portraying. Because some important details are left out, the boys and girls must explore what Mrs. Crickle-Crackle might do in circumstances that they imagine. During the improvised segment of the lesson, the group then creates a drama of their own. In the extension of the lesson, writing grows quite naturally from movement and drama.

Mrs. Crickle-Crackle

Crickle-crackle, spindle-shanks,
Won't say please and won't say thanks.
Her face is sour with a long thin nose.

She walks stiff-legged wherever she goes.
Sharp pointed elbows poke in and out.
If you get in her way, she'll give you a clout.
Her fingers prod and poke and pry.
Better look out or she'll make you cry.
                                    —Jean Cunningham

Explorations

After reading the poem to the class, the teacher asks questions like
the following to help the children fill in details about Mrs. Crickle-
Crackle:

How would Mrs. Crickle-Crackle's hands look? Can you make
your hands look like Mrs. Crickle-Crackle's?

Can you poke, and prod, and pry with your elbows? Make a
crooked shape before you poke, and prod, and pry. Make a
balanced shape.

How would Mrs. Crickle-Crackle walk?

Can you put on a face like Mrs. Crickle-Crackle?

Can you try to walk in two different ways so that your elbows
and fingers and knees are stiff?

How does Mrs. Crickle-Crackle bend down when she wants
something on the floor? Try bending in two ways.

When the children have worked out a mime for Mrs. Crickle-
Crackle, they are ready to make up a story about her. They should
be given time to try out the possibilities. The teacher can help them
by posing questions like:

What if you met Mrs. Crickle-Crackle on the way from school—
what would happen?

What if a policeman came just as Mrs. Crickle-Crackle was pok-
ing and prying—what would happen?

Suppose Mrs. Crickle-Crackle were a teacher—what might
happen?

The children work in groups of three or four to start developing dramatic improvisations. After each group has selected a situation, the teacher once more helps in the exploration of movement possibilities. If, for example, a group have settled on a situation involving a policeman, they would explore the policeman's movements. The teacher would then ask questions like:

Does your policeman walk or does he come in a car?

Two of you form a car together.

Try to form a car another way.

What does your policeman do to you? To Mrs. Crickle-Crackle? Is he holding a billy club? What does your policeman say to you?

What does Mrs. Crickle-Crackle do to the policeman?

Improvisation

The children now put the two explorations together in an improvised drama. They will need more time to create a story after their initial explorations. Later they can share the results with the rest of the class on a voluntary basis.

Extending the Lesson

After they have improvised a drama, the children are ready to write stories about Mrs. Crickle-Crackle and draw pictures to go along with them. Some children are able to imagine what Mrs. Crickle-Crackle would do in another situation, as figure 21 demonstrates.

LESSON 8: MONSTER

Many young children imagine that a monster is in the closet or down in the basement. The monster, an embodiment of a fear that children do not know how to deal with, disappears when child and parent investigate the spot together. Improvised movement can also help alleviate children's fears. The children make a monster with their own bodies, later drawing pictures of what they imagined.

A good way to start the lesson is to give the group a chance to talk about monsters—their fears about monsters, what they imagine

Leslie

One day my dad and I went to the store there was a big croud around the store door and there was a old lady there was a pin on her coat that said Mrs. Crickle Crackle she pushed and shoved, her elbows pointed. And she walked So straight.

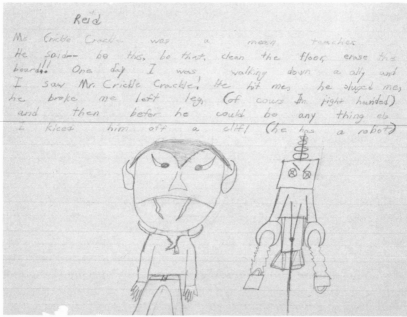

Reid

Mr Crickle Crackle was a mean teacher He said— be this, be that, clean the floor, erase the board!! One day I was walking down a ally and I saw Mr. Crickle Crackle! He hit me, he slugged me, he broke me left leg, (of cours I'm right handed) and then befor he could be any thing els I kices him off a cliff (he has a robot)

Figure 21. Illustrations and compositions done after the improvisation in a lesson on "Mrs. Crickle-Crackle."

112

their monsters look like, anecdotes about monsters. After the discussion, the teacher tells the children, "I'm going to help make you into monsters. First, I'll put you into an expansion chamber to soften you and make you large. Then the compression chamber of my machine will make you small and hard." The children then explore this monster-making process.

Exploration

THE EXPANSION CHAMBER
The children will achieve more variety if the teacher suggests:

Hold hands facing each other in a group of three or four. Continue to hold hands as you step backwards. Make that size grow larger and then smaller.

Find two ways for your group to expand and shrink, using up-and-down as well as in-out motions.

When each one of you has made as big a shape as you can, show that you are now "soft" by relaxing your body. I will "test" you. (The teacher can enter into the fun by "holding" an imaginary instrument to test the "softness.")

THE COMPRESSION CHAMBER
The group is now ready to be squeezed and hardened. To encourage varied explorations, the teacher may suggest:

Find three ways to shrink individually.

Find three ways to shrink as a group.

One group becomes the "manufacturer." Standing near another group, they tell the others what to do.

When all are satisfied with the "product," harden (freeze). I will test you.

Improvisation

The children now improvise their own monsters, still working in groups. First they "expand" (gradually getting larger) and then

Figure 22. Two examples of monsters that children drew after completing the lesson on *monsters*.

"shrink." As in all other improvisations, the teacher may need to remind the groups to use the ideas they tried during explorations.

Accompaniment

Bands one and four on Pink Floyd's *The Dark Side of the Moon* (Harvest, Gramophone, 1973) make an excellent accompaniment for this contemporary monster. The first selection on the disc,

"Speak to Me," begins with a loud, powerful heartbeat, which is particularly effective when the creature is being "made."

Extending the Lesson

The children are now ready to draw pictures of monsters. The two shown in figure 22 were drawn by a second grade class. The children will also want to hear a good story about monsters. Here are a number of excellent selections:

Grahame, Kenneth. *The Reluctant Dragon*, New York: Holiday House, 1938.

Mahy, Margaret. *The Dragon of an Ordinary Family*, New York: Franklin Watts, 1969.

Mayer, Mercer. *Professor Wormpup in Search of the Zapperoo*, New York: Golden Press, 1968.

Mayer, Mercer. *There's a Nightmare in My Closet*, New York: Golden Press, 1968.

Sendak, Maurice. *Where the Wild Things Are*, New York: Harper & Row, 1968.

LESSON 9: "VISIT"

The poem in this lesson generally interests young children because it was written by a child and because it was really published. The expressive movement lesson interests teachers for other reasons; for one, the meaning of the word *stealthy* is clarified through the children's response. In a follow-up lesson, the children use their experience for creative writing.

VISIT

I saw it come across our lawn.
It had silently
stealthily
climbed our wall
and now stood
like a statue of stone
dressed in dark and mystery.
The air was old.
　　　　　—Eve Recht, Age 11
　　　　　　Australia

Exploration

There are several ways to introduce this lesson. One way calls for the children to become weird, mysterious "statues." They may assume positions in which they balance themselves on one or both feet, or on an arm and a foot, while trying a variety of shapes. The teacher can encourage variation by calling for shapes that are stretched, twisted, small, or large. The lesson may also begin with casting shadows of body shapes onto the wall, using a flashlight or a lighted candle. The shapes, at first stationary, later move slowly from position to position. The movement will be freer and more interesting if other lights are turned low or completely out and a few flashlights placed around the room to create an eerie effect.

On a signal from the teacher, the children begin moving. The teacher can encourage variety by suggesting that the children find at least two well-defined shapes close to the ground. Variety in movement will also be encouraged with explorations like:

Move in different directions very slowly (forward, backward, to your sides, etc.).

Move very slowly with different parts of your body leading (head, elbow, knees).

Move at different speeds (very slowly, very fast). Change from slow to fast suddenly.

Freeze when the sound stops. Each time you start, move at a different level.

Improvisation

The children now create their own improvised dances using the shapes and the slow, stealthy movements they have explored. They may need reminders to use all their explorations.

Extending the Lesson

After the children have improvised a sequence around the mysterious figure coming across the lawn, they are ready to verbalize their ideas in poems or short stories. Their efforts are likely to be successful because they have explored the experience during the movement lesson and have had adequate time to mull over the ideas from several vantage points. The teacher can help the children express their ideas more fully by assisting them as they associate words like the following with their actions:

move stealthily   creep
drift   shift

The children will need time to write and edit their work. Most important, they will also need an audience. Poems should be placed on the bulletin board or "published" in book form, in a class magazine, or class newspaper.

The following poems were written by children from several groups after they had completed a lesson around "Visit":

> The mysterious shadow
> drifted across the lawn as
> The cat, a frozen statue,
> Stood poised to jump.
> > —Evan, 3rd Grade

> It appeared suddenly
> Over the wall
> I watched in the dark
> As it shifted shape
> Slowly, stealthily.
> My breath was gone.
> > —Chris, 3rd Grade

> Slowly, stealthily the shape
> Drifted across my window,
> A long shadow
> In the moonlight.
> > —Beth, 3rd Grade

LESSON 10: "JACK AND THE BEANSTALK"

Folk tales are important literary experiences for young children for a number of reasons. They meet children's emotional and intellectual needs, and they are part of our cultural heritage. Perhaps most important, when children hear folk tales they are intrigued. Indeed, they often seem mesmerized.

A tale that children especially enjoy is "Jack and the Beanstalk," the story of a poor boy who throws a seed on the ground one day and finds a giant beanstalk in its place the next morning. When he climbs the stalk, he has a series of exciting adventures as he is nearly caught by the ravenous giant who repeats, whenever Jack is near:

Fee, Fie, Foe, Fum,
I smell the blood
Of an Englishman.

A fine version of the tale for storytelling or reading is *Jack and the Beanstalk*, by Joseph Jacobs (New York: Walck, 1975). There are also many others that will be effective.

In translating the story into a dance-drama, most of the details are pared away to eliminate confusion. A few actions by the main characters make up the body of the story. Jack climbs the beanstalk and runs to the giant's castle, where he goes through the door and jumps into the oven to hide. The giant looks for Jack but soon falls asleep. Jack crawls out of the oven, steals the bag of gold, and retraces his steps around, across, and over the countryside, down the beanstalk, and home.

Exploration

The teacher should help the children explore each of the actions suggested in the story, always emphasizing trying out several ways to move. Some possibilities are suggested below.

CLIMBING
Find a starting position that shows you are about to start climbing.

Work on climbing action, standing in the spot. Lift your foot high, at the same time reach and pull with your arms. Use considerable force—pull hard!

PATHWAY
You have now climbed up the bean stalk. Off in the distance is a castle. Walk along the path to go there. You will have to zigzag here and there, and turn around. Don't forget to jump over the tree stumps in your way.

Now we have arrived in the giant's land. We have to run very fast to his castle.

MIME HIDING IN THE OVEN
Go into the castle very quickly.

Hide behind some furniture. Then dart quickly to another hiding place and another.

Get into the oven quickly. Find two ways to make yourself very small.

REVERSE ACTION

Now the giant is gone. You are to get out of the oven and steal the gold.

Run and jump and retrace the pathway to climb down the beanstalk. Retrace the same pathway you used coming to the castle. Dart from one hiding place to another.

GIANT

Now all of you are the giant. You take thumping strides around the castle, looking for Jack.

Put on your boots. Pull hard. They are BIG. Show me how the giant walks. Make your steps bigger, heavier, and travel to different parts of the floor.

You are tired. Show me how you make a big yawn, stretch, and settle down to sleep.

ACCOMPANIMENT

As the children climb up the beanstalk, the teacher counts to 8 or 10, slowly. While the children devise pathways, the teacher slowly beats a tambourine. To accompany the giant's strides, the teacher uses a drum. Alternatively, the children can tell and replay their own versions of the story on tape.

Improvisation

The children work in groups of two. One child is the giant, the other Jack. All go through the pantomime making up their own versions of the story. The teacher must encourage variations.

Extending the Lesson

Teachers can help children relate movement experience to language by having them retell the story in their own words. If the stories are tape-recorded, they can be used as accompaniment for the improvisations. The class can compare their versions with one of the following:

Chase, Richard, *Jack Tales*. Boston: Houghton Mifflin, 1948.
Still, James, *Jack and the Wonder Beans*. New York: Putnam's, 1977.

Comparing different versions of the story will give the children insight into the way folk tales are constructed. They will then be ready to write their own "Jack and the Beanstalk" stories.

BIBLIOGRAPHY: ADDITIONAL REFERENCES FOR THE PRIMARY GRADES

Stories and Poems Suited to Improvisation

Anonymous. "The Squirrel." In *Feather and Fur*, edited by Grete Mannheim, New York: Knopf, 1967.

Aruego, Jose. *Look What I Can Do*. New York: Scribner's, 1971.

Carle, Eric. *Do You Want To Be My Friend?* New York: Crowell, 1971.

Carle, Eric. *The Tiny Seed*. New York: Crowell, 1970.

Carle, Eric. *The Very Hungry Caterpillar*. Cleveland: World, 1972.

de Regniers, Beatrice Schenck. *May I Bring a Friend?* New York: Atheneum, 1964.

Edey, Marion, & Grider, Dorothy. "Trot Along, Pony." In *Time for Poetry*, edited by May Hill Arbuthnot and Shelton Root. Glenview, Ill.: Scott, Foresman, 1968.

Kuskin, Karla. "The Balloon." In *Piping Down the Valleys Wild*, edited by Nancy Larrick. New York: Delacorte, 1968.

Kuskin, Karla. "Tiptoe." In *Time for Poetry*, edited by May Hill Arbuthnot and Shelton Root. Glenview, Ill.: Scott, Foresman, 1968.

Sendak, Maurice. *Where the Wild Things Are*. New York: Harper & Row, 1963.

Udry, Janet. *The Moon Jumpers*. New York: Harper & Row, 1959.

Sources on Developing Movement Around Language and Literature

Boorman, Joyce. *Creative Dance in the Primary Grades*. Don Mills, Ontario: Longmans, 1970.

Boorman, Joyce. *Dance and Language Experiences with Children*. Don Mills, Ontario: Longmans, 1973.

Bruce, Valerie. *Dance and Dance Drama in Education*. London: Pergamon Press, 1965.

North, Marion. *Movement Education*. New York: Dutton, 1973.

Sheehy, Emma D. *Children Discover Music and Dance*. New York: Teachers College Press, 1968.

7

Improvisations:
The Intermediate Years

Teachers who try improvisation with children between the ages of nine and twelve for the first time find that initial reactions vary greatly. Some classes love movement lessons immediately. Others need coaxing and can only be led to enjoy the work after the teacher has developed a relationship of friendship and trust with them and worked steadily and sensitively on basic ideas.

GETTING UNDER WAY

Because children in this age group have a lot of physical energy, the sensible place to begin is with improvisation preceded by jumping practice, which taxes the boys and girls physically. Most of the movement lessons in this chapter meet the need for physical activity. They are simple and demand an energetic interpretation. There is also a great deal of room for expansion and subtlety, which the teacher and children can add as they begin to get the "feel" of expressive movement.

Sometimes one or two children in the class cannot bring themselves to try movement. Rather than force the issue, the teacher is wise to let them participate doing something else, perhaps the accompaniment. Even the shyest will soon become skilled in percussion or in lighting. If all else fails, these few children should be allowed to read in the library until they wish to stay with their class of their own accord.

CONDUCTING THE MOVEMENT LESSON

As with younger children, the teacher must be especially careful to observe what the children are doing, for their improvised dances will reveal what they understand. These are important questions to keep in mind while observing:

- Have the children grasped the *main idea*?
- Have they understood the *story line*, *characters*, *setting*, and *mood* of the selection?
- Have they responded to the *rhythm* of the selection?
- Does their interpretation evoke the *imagery* suggested by the poem or story?

It is important also to consider: *In what ways can I help strengthen the quality and range of the children's movement without spoiling their ideas?*

For observation of this kind, the teacher needs to use movement analysis to make judgments based on **how**, **what**, and **where** of the movement. Skill involved in such observation grows quickly and has the great virtue of providing concrete help while building on the child's own movement preferences.

Perhaps because children in this age group are especially self-conscious, it is important to set a serious tone in the intermediate classroom. Teachers should make it clear from the outset that movement is a school subject and that children are expected to learn something during the lesson. The best way to achieve this objective is to tell the class what you want them to learn before you start and once again after the lesson is done. Make it clear that you expect full cooperation and effort, and set standards for good behavior. Boys and girls in these grades respond more positively if in their perception the work they do is meaningful.

LESSON 1: "ROADS"

In "Roads," the poet chooses a few words to draw an impressionistic picture that is saturated with feelings and associations. The poem makes travel highly appealing with a few concrete references that suggest all sorts of adventures. The details suggested by the words in the poem are filled in by the children as they mime their versions of the exotic things and people one meets in travels to faraway places. The road is symbolized by the pathways created by the children, who clarify imagery in the process.

Roads

A road might lead to anywhere—
   To harbor towns and quays,
Or to a witch's pointed house
   Hidden by bristly trees.
It might lead past the tailor's door,
   Where he sews with needle and thread,
Or by Miss Pim the milliner's,
   With her hats for every head.
It might be a road to a great, dark cave
   With treasures and gold piled high,
Or a road with a mountain tied to its end,
   Blue-humped against the sky.
Oh, a road might lead you anywhere—
   To Mexico or Maine.
But then, it might just fool you, and—
   Lead you back home again!
              —Rachel Field

Explorations

MIME

After listening to the poem, the children pair off to mime actions that suggest:

A witch or witch's house
The tailor sewing
Miss Pim, the milliner
A great dark cave
A blue-humped mountain.

The teacher can help the children think of many different ways to do their pantomimes by suggesting ideas like the following:

Can you make your body crooked?
Can you make an ugly face like a witch?

The children usually can easily mime a witch (see figure 23), but they do not know how tailors used to sew (by hand) or what a

Figure 23. The children mime the witch and her house, during a lesson on "Roads."

milliner is. The teacher will, therefore, have to help them define the words. The mountain and the cave (see figure 24), on the other hand, are always understood by the boys and girls. The children interpret both of these objects imaginatively, especially if the teacher asks questions like:

> Can you find two ways to make a cave?
> Two of you stand together to make a cave.
> Make a cave by yourself.

The children will need time to develop their ideas.

ROAD AND PATHWAYS
Still working in pairs, one person becomes the traveler; the other sits still with ample space around him or her. The following ideas will help the travelers develop individual, varied "roads" or floor pathways:

Figure 24. The children mime a great dark cave, during "Roads."

Move around the people who are sitting down when you hear the tambourine shake. Stop when I bang the tambourine and return "home" (back to your original partner) by the quickest route.

Set out on your "road" again. Try to notice which children you go around, in front of, and behind. Freeze when I hit the tambourine and go straight "home."

Practice until you can repeat the same "road" in both directions.

Try skipping (running, hopping, etc.) as you leave "home." Use very big steps when you return.

Change places with your partner.

Improvisation

The travelers now begin their journeys as the poem is used as accompaniment. At appropriate points, the people sitting on the floor perform the mimes they have practiced; the travelers also mime scenes as they stop on their "roads." At the end of the poem, perhaps at the line "Oh, a road might lead you anywhere," the children move quickly to get back "home" to their original partner.

Extending the Lesson

Many poets have written about roads and imagined that one led to something special for them. The children may enjoy hearing other ideas about roads and may want to talk about where they themselves have traveled. A good poem for comparison with Rachel Field's "Roads" is this one:

Roadways

One road leads to London,
One road leads to Wales.
My road leads me seaward
To the white dipping sails.

My road calls me, lures me.
West, east, south and north;
Most roads lead men homewards,
My road leads me forth.
—John Masefield

LESSON 2: "GET UP, BLUES"

This poem contrasts sharply drawn images and moods. While children cannot and should not analyze the poem for its many patterns, they can, through the movement lesson, easily grasp the contrasts between the sad and happy moods it expresses.

Get Up, Blues

Blues
Never climb a hill
Or sit on a roof
in starlight.

Blues
Just bend low
And moan in the street
And shake a borrowed cup.

Blues
Just sit around
sipping,
Hatching yesterdays.

Get up, Blues.
Fly.
Learn what it means
To be up high.
—James A. Emanuel

Explorations

The group first looks through the poem to locate words that describe sad and happy moods, later adding more of their own. The teacher next asks, "How do people move when they are happy? When they are sad?" The children will offer many ideas. Some possibilities of both kinds of words are listed in Table 6.

Table 6. Mood and Movement Words for "Get Up, Blues"

Mood Words		Movement Words	
Sad	*Happy*	*Sad*	*Happy*
low	high	bending low	flying
downcast	up	sinking	jumping
miserable	enthusiastic	slouching	leaping
sad	joyful	sitting around	running
gloomy	quick	dragging	reaching
glum	laughing	limping	cartwheeling
heavy	elated	collapsing	spinning
dark	merry		
slow	glad		
	carefree		

The words suggested by the children are now used for exploration. To help the boys and girls express the first mood, the teacher might suggest:

You are sad. Find a position that shows how you feel. Show that you are sad in the following positions: standing, kneeling, sitting, lying.

Link two of the positions together by moving very slowly from one to the other.

Find a partner. With your partner create a "depressed" position.

Develop a sequence that begins with partners back to back and finishes with each facing the other. In the middle part of your sequence, travel from one spot to another. Remember to express your sadness through your body.

In explorations of movement for the second mood, the teacher might make the following suggestions:

Walk, increasing the speed of your walk until you break into a run. (Watch for spacing.)

Run. When there is room, jump in any direction. Repeat jumping, this time as high as possible. (To look as if you are jumping very high, tuck your feet under you.)

From a standing position, jump high in the air, using your arms to show that you are bursting with energy. While jumping, shout something which shows that you are happy.

Try running and jumping in at least two different ways. Take turns with a partner.

With your partner, find two ways to spin.

Improvisation

Working individually, with a partner or in a small group, the children can now devise a sequence contrasting moods. The teacher should caution the group to make the differences between moods very clear through body movement, as well as through starting and finishing shapes.

Extending the Lesson

The words in the poem and the lists made by the class may be used to express the children's own moods. The children first talk about times when they themselves feel happy or sad. After sharing their ideas, they write about their own feelings, perhaps using the words explored in the movement lesson.

LESSON 3: "THE TERM"

Although this poem is deceptively simple, children do not always understand the meaning of the title or the comparison between a rumpled sheet of paper and a man. The lesson that follows provides a setting for improvising a dance around a crumpled sheet of brown paper and a man. The movement and follow-up writing help children understand the comparison more clearly.

The Term

> A rumpled sheet
> of brown paper
> about the length
>
> and apparent bulk
> of a man was
> rolling with the
>
> wind slowly over
> and over in
> the street as
>
> a car drove down
> upon it and
> crushed it to
>
> the ground. Unlike
> a man it rose
> again rolling
>
> with the wind over
> and over to be as
> it was before.
> —William Carlos Williams

Explorations

A good way to start this lesson is to give the pupils large sheets of paper which they crush into any shape they desire. The children then lie on the floor in a shape like the crushed paper and from that position explore rolling on the floor. Directions like the following will help them become inventive:

> Vary the level of your rolls so that some are higher than others. ("Log," shoulder, and tucked-up side rolls can all be done slowly and without discomfort on a hard floor.)
>
> Practice spinning on your tummy or seat to help vary the speed and direction of your movement.
>
> Practice continuous movement that includes rolls, spins, and turns on your feet, as well as close to the floor.
>
> When I bang the drum, freeze in whatever position you find yourself.
>
> Vary direction, moving sideways and backward, as well as forward (upward and downward).

Figure 25. During a lesson on "The Term," the children break the continuity of their movement by holding themselves still in a balanced position from time to time.

Vary your speed, sometimes moving slowly, sometimes fast.

Break the continuity or flow of your movement by holding yourself still in a balanced position from time to time. Find two ways to stop. (See figure 25.)

Improvisation

Before the children put together an improvised movement sequence, they should discuss what would happen to a sheet of paper and what would happen to a man after being run over by a car. Half the class becomes the brown paper and the other children represent the man, as all develop sequences in which they roll in ways suggested during the exploration.

The teacher should emphasize that a movement contrast is needed as the car runs over the paper. (Children usually think that rolls should be followed by a sudden strong movement, flattening and collapsing. See figure 26.) After all have flattened and collapsed, only those who are "the brown paper" continue rolling.

Figure 26. During "The Term" the children often think that the rolls should be followed by a sudden, strong movement of flattening and collapsing.

This improvisation can be developed with music of the children's choice. A popular tune that allows for movement of various speeds and that has a lyrical quality would be a good choice. And a heavy drum beat for the sudden flattening and collapsing movements will enhance the contrast with the more flowing, lighter rolling and turning.

Extending the Lesson

The children now write their own poems comparing dissimilar things, such as:

> Fireworks and lightning
> An airplane and a butterfly
> String puppets and real people

A seventh-grade group supplied the following list of words for a poem about fireworks and lightning:

crackles	strikes	brilliant
zooms	sputters	flashes
flutters	growls	white

Then they "brainstormed" the poem itself.

> Like lightning
> The firework
> Strikes the air
> Exploding
> In a white, crackling flash.
> Unlike lightning,
> The firework flutters,
> Twisting and turning,
> Growling and sputtering,
> To the ground.
> > —A 7th-Grade Class
> > East Lansing, Michigan

LESSON 4: "HIST WHIST"

This poem uses sounds that strongly suggest the quick scuttling movements of small creatures like mice and "ghost things." Youngsters usually enjoy and understand the onomatopoeia as well as the mildly frightening experience with ghosts, goblins, and witches produced by the lesson.

Hist Whist

hist whist
little ghostthings
tip-toe
twinkle-toe

little twitchy
witches and tingling
goblins
hob-a-nob   hob-a-nob

little hoppy happy
toad in tweeds
little itchy mousies

with scuttling
eyes rustle and run and
hidehidehide
whist

whisk look out for the old woman
with the wart on her nose
what she'll do to yer
nobody knows

for she knows the devil ooch
the devil ouch
the devil
ach the great

green
dancing
devil
devil

devil
devil   wheeEEE

—e. e. cummings

Sound Effects

Sound effects will add considerable excitement to the interpretation. Here are a few suggestions that will help children create dramatic accompaniments.

> With a partner, make sounds a "ghost thing" might make passing you by. Repeat: Hob-a-nob . . . Hist-whist . . . Twitchy-witches.
>
> Make up two words of your own with lots of "s" and "t" and "sh" and "ch" sounds. Add sound effects with your hands and fingernails, rubbing or scratching or tapping against the floor or your body.
>
> Work out a simple pattern on drums and cymbals to accompany the different parts of the poem.
>
> Work out a plan for choral reading of the poem itself.
>
> In groups of four, make a "sound track" (with a tape recorder) using percussion, your fingers, or anything else you think appropriate for the poem. We can use the sound track later as a background for movement.

Lighting Effects

Mini-flashlights switched on and off by the children make effective lighting. A green floodlight plugged into the wall can highlight the devil dance. The children, holding the mini-flashlights, will need a chance to practice working their lights before the improvisation.

Explorations

GHOST THINGS, TWITCHY WITCHES, AND HAPPY TOAD

The teacher will help the children develop varied movements with directions like:

Listen to the tambourine (use short bursts of light, quick shakes with fairly long stops). Freeze when I bang the tambourine strongly. (Repeat, placing stress on freezing, which is sudden but controlled.)

While in a sitting position, make your hands into a variety of shapes moving from place to place in the space all around you. Bring your elbows, wrists, and fingers into the action. Make your hands twitch in the same tempo as the words "hob-a-nob," "scuttle."

Half the class, spread out on the floor. The other half, hide behind a partner. When the tambourine shakes, the hidden partners make quick, darting gestures with their arms above, to the side, or close to their partner's feet. (To help the children make strange, sudden actions, give them ample practice.)

Directions like the following will help:

Twist your hands.
Twist your arms.
Twist your wrists.

When I bang the tambourine, make your hand disappear. *Really fast now.*

Now we will extend quick movement to the whole body. Each time I bang the tambourine, the person who is hiding moves at lightning speed behind someone else and freezes in a high or low position when the sound stops.

Those standing still, spin when you hear the tambourine sound and freeze to make a joint "shape" with each new partner. Make each "shape" at a different level with angular or curved outlines.

The children will use more variation in shape if the teacher emphasizes different parts of the body (i.e., hands, knees, elbow, feet) and gives time for half of the class to watch the other half.

When I bang my tambourine, make a shape close to the floor.

Next time make a shape stretching your body as high as possible.

Twist your body to the right (or left).

With a partner develop some movement ideas that contrast "hoppy happy toad" and "little itchy mousies."

Practice "hoppy happy toad" with very high jumps from two feet, landing very quickly and in a deep crouch position.

DANCING DEVIL

The following directions will help the children develop ideas about the dancing devil:

Make a long jump, landing in a wide position, with feet and arms spread.

Continue to run afterwards. (The children will need practice working for controlled landings.)

With half of the group watching, try a different kind of jump making a shape in the air before landing.

The teacher can help the youngsters achieve variety in jumps with directions like the following:

When you are in the air, try different ways to tuck your feet under your body.

Try jumping so that when you are in the air your feet are wide apart.

Bend close to the ground and hammer the floor with your fists; when you hear the cymbals crash, leap into the air, fists high above your head.

Make a high, wide jump, landing with feet and arms outspread.

Practice landing heavily, but without hurting your feet, and face different directions every time you jump.

Practice running and jumping. Make your jump so high that you can "kick" the air before your hand.

Stamp your feet on the ground very quickly. Then hammer the floor with your fists.

Take a partner and hammer the floor. Then do a strong, high jump in the air in unison.

Work out a gesture that would suggest the casting of a spell.

Improvisation

Several possible sequences may be developed. Any may be selected as long as two sharply different characters provide simple but dramatic differences in movement. Some possibilities for the improvisation are:

Half the class can be "ghost things," the other half "dancing devils," each taking the floor in turn.

Half the class freezes, becoming a focus for the others to move around.

"Ghost-things" can be subdivided into ghosts, witches, toads, and mice. Each develops individual movement characteristics and each is highlighted briefly before the whole group moves together.

The dancing devils could be a few children who are about to pounce on mice and toads.

A sequence can be made by combining jumping, hammering, leaping, and gesturing.

Extending the Lesson

After completing the movement lesson for "Hist Whist," classroom discussion could lead in a number of directions. The teacher may, for instance, wish to explore some of the sounds or words in the poem further. Questions like the following will help the children think about the words in the poem:

What words suggest nervousness and fear?

Why does the poem say "ooch," "ouch," "ach" after the word devil?

Are there any words that make you think the goblins, "ghost things," witches, toads, and mice move in quick, jerky movements? Why?

An interesting discussion can also grow from a comparison between "Hist Whist" and Robert Herrick's poem "The Hag" (in *A Young American's Book of English Poetry*, edited by Shirley Marshall. New York: Washington Square Press, 1967).

Children always find ghosts and witches fascinating. The following books will therefore prove interesting to them.

Babbitt, Natalie. *The Devil's Storybook*. New York: Doubleday, 1974.

Brewton, Sara & John. *Shrieks at Night: Macabre Poems, Eerie and Humorous*. New York: Crowell, 1969.

Garfield, Leon. *Mister Corbett's Ghost*. New York: Pantheon, 1968.

Garfield, Leon. *The Ghost Downstairs*. New York: Pantheon, 1969.

Hunter, Mollie. *The Ghost of Glencoe*. New York: Funk and Wagnalls, 1969.

Leodhas, Sorche Nic. *Ghosts Go Haunting*. New York: Holt, Rinehart and Winston, 1965.

Leodhas, Sorche Nic. *Twelve Great Cats and Other Eerie Scottish Tales*. New York: Dutton, 1971.

Lines, Kathleen. *House of Nightmares*. New York: Farrar, Straus and Giroux, 1968.

Preussler, Otfried. *The Satanic Mill*. New York: Macmillan, 1973.

Singer, Isaac Bashevis. *The Fearsome Inn*. New York: Scribner's, 1967.

Sleator, William. *Blackbriar*. New York: Dutton, 1972.

LESSON 5: "WILD IRON"

Rhythm is a pervasive feature of all poems, in fact, of all human activities. In the evocative poem featured in this lesson, the sea pounding against the shore provides an insistent, powerful beat. Children are quick to respond to the strong rhythm of the poem spontaneously, but without the teacher's help, they may not capture the violence, the weight, the force of the sea. To achieve strength and power in the children's movement, emphasis in the lesson therefore should be on **how** the children move.

Wild Iron

Sea go dark, dark with wind.
Feet go heavy, heavy with sand.
Thoughts go wild, wild with the sound
Of iron on the old shed swinging and clanging.
Go dark, go heavy, go wild, go round
  Dark with wind
  Heavy with sand
Wild with the iron that tears
  at the nail
And the foundering shriek of the gale.

               —Allen Curnow

The teacher will have to assess carefully the ability of the class to work in groups for this lesson. A class with considerable experience in expressive movement can work in groups of six or seven. Less experienced children will be more successful in groups of three or four.

Accompaniment

The poem read by a single choral group or in canon style is the best accompaniment. At first, however, the teacher should use a drum or tambourine to help children become aware of the poem's rhythmic quality. When the children interpret the poem orally, they must all maintain the same rhythm as they build the volume and tempo to a crescendo, which climaxes at the end of the poem. A clashing sound of a cymbal is an excellent way to reinforce the final buildup.

During the movement interpretation, the poem should be read again while the teacher reinforces the rhythm with a drum beat, which gradually builds to a crescendo.

Exploration

STEPPING
The teacher helps the children explore the first two lines of the poem, which are spoken rhythmically and relatively slowly.

Sea go dark, dark with wind.
Feet go heavy, heavy with sand.

A drum can also emphasize the rhythm. Instructions like the following help the group try out their own variations:

Step without moving very far.

You are moving with heavy steps. You can hardly lift your foot as you try to make different kinds of steps. Make an imaginary pattern without moving very far. You can put your heel on the ground very firmly, walking flat-footed. Find your own way of making footprints.

Try making footprints while moving in different directions, going sideways (forward, backward).

Gradually make the steps larger, as you move your body in preparation for the next stage.

SWINGING

Still maintaining the rhythm of the poem, the children start a swinging action by shifting their weight from one foot to the other when they hear:

Thoughts go wild, wild with the sound
of iron on the old shed swinging and clanging.

They should keep knees relaxed and try going forward and backward, from side to side. Suggestions by the teacher could include:

As soon as your feet have picked up the rhythm, let your arms swing to make the movement bigger.

Give your swing a feeling of heaviness and make the action as large as you can. Keep your knees resilient so that you get the feel of the swing.

WHIRLING AND TURNING

The children start whirling when they hear the next three lines:

> Go dark, go heavy, go wild, go round
> Dark with wind
> Heavy with sand

To avoid becoming dizzy, the children should spin a short way in one direction, changing direction after a moment or two. As they whirl, the teacher should remind them to keep their space and maintain a feeling of resilience in their feet and knees. Their arms should be outstretched for balance.

LEAPING

The movement climaxes at the conclusion of the poem:

> Wild with the iron that tears
>   at the nail
> And the foundering shriek of the gale.

The children leap high into the air, turning while they jump. The teacher can help them achieve variation, height, and length in their jumps with the following directions:

Leap from one foot to the other, with a slight turn in the air. Now leap from your other foot. Repeat a few times, working for continuity and flow.

Run and jump into the air, working for height. Fling your arms high.

Crouch close to the ground before beginning your jumps for a strong thrust. Try crouching in a different position. Practice high jumps, turning and leaping from one foot to another.

Turn your head in the direction toward which you jump before you begin to turn while jumping.

Improvisation

The class works in groups or as a whole, developing a sequence that includes stepping, turning, and leaping. The teacher should help the children with starting and finishing positions and with the transitions from one action to another.

Extending the Lesson

A follow-up discussion about the poem and its rhythm will prove rewarding. The children could compare "Wild Iron" with other sea poems, like "The Main-Deep," or with music about the sea, such as Debussy's *La Mer* (Eugene Ormandy and the Philadelphia Orchestra, Columbia, MG30950).

The Main-Deep

The long rolling,
Steady-pouring,
Deep-trenchéd
Green billow:

The wide-topped,
Unbroken,
Green-glacid,
Slow-sliding.

Cold-flushing,
On—on—on—
Chill-rushing,
Hush-hushing,

Hush—hushing. . . .
—James Stephens

The following picture books have excellent pictures of the sea:

Hodges, Margaret. *The Wave*. Boston: Houghton Mifflin, 1964.
Tresselt, Alvin. *Hide and Seek Fog*. New York: Lothrop, Lee, and Shepard, 1965.

LESSON 6: THE SPACE SHIP

Because of "Star Trek," "Battle Star Galactica," "Star Wars," and other television shows and movies, space adventures have caught the imagination of today's children. In the lesson that follows we tap this enormous source of vivid imagery in the interest of language and movement. During the improvisation, the children create a "happening," an event in which they enact entry into the atmosphere, cruising, landing on an alien planet, and exploring it.

Later, the teacher leads the children into writing activities. Writing is likely to be enhanced because children are readily caught up in the imaginary experience with the space ship and the details of space travel.

A good way to begin the lesson is to talk about favorite scenes from films or television programs, gradually bringing the discussion to the kinds of words and images needed for a dramatized space story. Ask the children for space ship jargon, descriptions of space ships and of landing procedures, ideas about planet exploration, names of planets, and similar material. Some possibilities are:

atmosphere	X-rays
life support	entry
U.F.O.'s	landing
alien	gravity
spaceship	Venus
10, 9, 8, 7, 6, 5, 4, 3, 2, 1	lift-off
oxygen	all systems go
freeze-dried food	meteors
space suit	atmosphere
galaxies	milky way
stars	Jupiter
planets	Saturn
sun	Mars

Explorations

The following framework divides movement into two phases. In phase 1, actions are linked to the flight and landing of the spaceship. In phase 2, the children investigate a planet.

PHASE 1

Here are exploratory movements to suggest for the flight and landing of the spaceship.

Preparing for Takeoff: Crouch down on your feet, keeping your back straight and your elbows bent so that your hands are pointing toward the ceiling.

Takeoff: As I beat the drum slowly six times, gradually move your arms upward. Bring your arms down on the seventh and eighth counts so that they can help you shoot upward into a very strong, stretched jump from both feet when the drum bangs. (Work for contrasts in speed and a full stretch in the jump.)

Cruising in space requires navigation, but not much apparent energy. Run quickly, smoothly, and very lightly, taking care to avoid each other. Use all the available floor space.

Space ships often move suddenly, then hover. We are going to practice moving very quickly for a short distance, and then running lightly while remaining in the same spot. After that, we will shoot off in a different direction. (Children will enjoy this if they are challenged to move quickly and then brake suddenly.)

Now come into a *landing*, very slowly and carefully. Turn and sink slowly. (Repeat and ask the class for suggestions on possible improvements. Children of this age group are quite capable of evaluating their own work.)

PHASE 2

A number of options are possible for reconnaissance of the planet. At first all the children should try a few ideas together; later they will develop their own individual detailed movements. Music makes an excellent accompaniment during both exploration and improvisation. The teacher can help the children explore the ideas with directions like:

With plenty of space around you, stand in a comfortable position and close your eyes. The planet is dark. You must feel around you with your hands and feet before stepping in any direction.

Take a partner. One of you closes your eyes. The other leads him or her on a short "journey," giving instructions on when to step over an imaginary object. Make sure you safeguard your partner from bumping into others.

Stay close to the ground and travel very slowly and cautiously. You "slip" and "fall" by collapsing and rolling, but then you recover and keep on moving. If you find yourself next to someone, go over or under the person without a word.

Once more on your feet, practice walking where there is not much gravity and you are nearly weightless.

Now the pull of gravity is very strong. It is a big effort to take every step. You have to pull very hard to lift your feet at all.

Improvisation

Ask the children to divide into groups of three. Each group will land on its own "planet" and work out its own version of phases 1 and 2. The journeys on the "planets" are made more interesting if only one of the group members sets out, leaving the other two sitting close together on the floor. Not only do the actions then become easily visible, but the stationary bodies form a useful focus to move around, toward, over, and away from. The explorers should have a limited time for their expeditions so that space ships can repeat the flight cycle and land on a second and third planet.

A considerable part of the planning can be left to the children, with lighting and accompaniment devised by individual groups. The children can develop their own movement details through discussion and observation. The teacher should encourage large, clear movement and contrasts in speed and effort to give exciting dynamics to the action and to help with transitions.

ACCOMPANIMENT

A drum and/or cymbals will be very useful for phase 1, especially for takeoff. For parts of both phases, music might be selected from recordings: For example: Suites from *Star Wars* and *Close Encounters of the Third Kind* (Zubin Mehta and the Los Angeles Philharmonic, London, ZM1001); *Diamonds Are Forever* (United Artists, ULK3015); *2001: A Space Odyssey* (Music from the Motion Picture Soundtrack, MGM Records S1E-13ST).

LIGHTING

If possible, use lighting for this lesson. Mini-flashlights will create "stars" in a darkened room, and ordinary flashlights can be used like searchlights. The "planets" can be produced by colored floodlights or by an overhead projector beamed over a dish of water that contains a little food coloring and a few drops of oil. These simple devices are well worth the small effort they entail.

Extending the Lesson

"Space Ship" offers several kinds of valuable resources to the young writer who wants to tell a story. The vocabulary, the names of the "planets," the discussion at the beginning of the lesson, and the improvisation itself can suggest possibilities for plots, characters, and settings. Writing that grows out of this lesson is frequently rich in detail and vitality.

The following books and stories will let the children explore space travel further:

Ballou, Arthur W. *Marooned in Orbit*. Boston: Little, Brown, 1968.
Bova, Benjamin. *End of Exile*. New York: Dutton, 1975.
Cameron, Eleanor. *The Wonder Flight to the Mushroom Planet*. Boston: Little, Brown, 1954.
Doyle, Arthur Conan. *The Lost World*. New York: Random House, 1959.
Engdahl, Sylvia Louise. *Enchantress from the Stars*. New York: Atheneum, 1970.
Engdahl, Sylvia Louise. *Journey between Worlds*. New York: Atheneum, 1970.
Fisk, Nicholas. *Grinny*. New York: Nelson, 1974.
Hoover, H. M. *The Rains of Eridan*. New York: V. King, 1977.
Karl, Jean. *The Turning Place: Stories of a Future Past*. New York: Dutton, 1976.
Pesek, Ludek. *The Earth Is Near*. New York: Bradbury, 1974.
Todd, Ruthven. *Space Cat*. New York: Scribner's, 1952.

LESSON 7: FIREWORKS

Fireworks is a subject that evokes vivid and exciting imagery involving both movement and sound. This lesson begins with a discussion and brainstorming session during which the class collects words, images, and sounds that are connected with fireworks. The children then help design a "fireworks display," read about fireworks, and write their own poems.

Typical words suggested by children during brainstorming are listed in Table 7.

Table 7. Words about Fireworks

Sounds	Actions	Miscellaneous
ssss. . . .	explode	bright colors
woosh	spin	dark sky
bang	shoot	patterns
whirr	shower	rockets
crack	drift	golden rain
spit-ps-ps	jump	firecrackers
ooh . . . aah	whirl	sparks
	spray	flowing

Exploration

Help children develop their own ideas through explorations as follows:

FIRECRACKERS
Find space on the floor and jump suddenly into a different space when you hear the tambourine bang. I am going to bang many times. Every time you hear the sound, jump into a new space as quickly as you can, changing directions each time.

CATHERINE WHEELS AND GOLDEN RAIN
Spin on the spot, arms outstretched for balance. Keep your knees bent and resilient.

Working with one or more partners, work out an opening and "bursting" action together, so that your firework opens slowly and then suddenly bursts. (See figures 27, 28, and 29.)

ROCKETS
Crouch low to the ground. The fuse is lit. When the cymbals clash, take off with a mighty jump, stretching your arms and legs as far as possible. (See figure 30.)

Figure 27. The children whirl in pairs during "Fireworks."

Figure 28. Here a group whirl like a firework that is exploding.

Figure 29. In a unique interpretation of fireworks, five members of a group make a shape on the floor as the sixth moves quickly around them.

Figure 30. During a lesson on *fireworks*, the children curl up in a position from which they can jump straight up.

Improvisation

The class breaks up into groups of four, five, or six children, each responsible for working out their own display complete with sounds. If there are enough percussion instruments, each group might like to combine verbal and percussion sounds.

While the children explore the possibilities for fireworks, the teacher moves from group to group, making suggestions. Children should be encouraged to work in unison, two or three at a time. Some may need to practice jumping explosively or whirling faster and faster.

After the groups have improvised their fireworks displays, they share them with the rest of the class.

Lighting Effects

If it is possible to darken the room and use mini-flashlights, the excitement and atmosphere will be greatly enhanced. An overhead projector in a darkened room will also create a semitheatrical light.

Extending the Lesson

James Reeves's poem "Fireworks" will feed the children's imaginations further. After hearing and discussing it, they should be ready to write their own descriptions of fireworks.

Fireworks

They rise like sudden fiery flowers
That burst upon the night.
Then fall to earth in burning showers
Of crimson blue and white.
Like buds too wonderful to name,
Each miracle unfolds
And catherine-wheels begin to flame
Like whirling marigolds.

—James Reeves

LESSON 8: ORION

Greek and other myths are important in our culture, appearing frequently in our vocabulary, literature, and history. The myths are

good stories, too, for they contain action, suspense, and basic con-
flicts. They will interest children especially if they are introduced
through dance-drama.

Many myths "explain" how the constellations were placed in the
sky. In the lesson that follows, children become acquainted with constellations and with Greek myths about them and then develop a
dance-drama, which tells the story of the constellation Orion.

The Astronomy Associated with Constellations

Work begins with an introduction to constellations and one or more
of the myths associated with them. The boys and girls can find constellations on a star chart and draw them on a sheet of paper. It will
be most interesting if the children can see picture representations as
well as the star patterns themselves. Such pictures might be found in
books or drawn by some children.

Constellations can also be depicted in tableau style by groups of
children placed around the room in the patterns made by the stars of
different constellations. Each star would be represented by one
child, so that the Big Dipper, for example, would be made up of
seven children. If the room is dark and each child carries a mini-
flashlight, the constellation pattern can be reflected on the ceiling,
more or less as it appears in the sky.

Myths Associated with Some Constellations

THE GREAT BEAR (REPRESENTED BY THE BIG DIPPER)
The Great Bear was put into the sky to tell earthly bears the
seasons. During the winter months when the group of stars is low in
the skies, it is time for earthly bears to keep warm and snug in their
dens. When the constellation is high in the sky, it is summer and the
bears' long sleep is over.

DRAGON
Draco, the Dragon, the guardian of the golden apples of the
Hesperides, was slain by Cadmus, who then planted half its teeth.
From the teeth, dragon men sprang up.

LEO, THE NEMEAN LION
Leo, the Nemean Lion, was killed by Hercules in the first of the

twelve "labors" he completed to meet the challenge of the king of Argos. The hero killed the lion by thrusting his arm down its throat. With difficulty he removed the tough skin, later wearing it as armor.

ORION

Orion was a great hunter who boasted that there was no animal on earth he could not overcome and kill. To punish Orion for his arrogance, Jupiter sent the deadly scorpion to sting him. The goddess Diana, herself a huntress, felt sorry for Orion and put him in the heavens, far away in the sky from the scorpion, who was also turned into a constellation.

Exploration for Orion

Once the children have heard the myths and learned something about the constellations, they are ready to interpret a myth that intrigues them. As an example, directions for a dance-drama about Orion are given here. Other schemes, of course, could be used.

The story is danced by two children representing three characters: Orion, who is proud and agile; Orion's prey, the hunted animal; and Scorpion, who is quick and has a distinctive shape. The children work in groups of two, taking each part in turn.

ORION AND PREY

Orion hunts and wrestles with a partner who later assumes Scorpion's role. The teacher will help the children explore the movement possibilities with tasks like the following:

Find two ways to run and jump (as if leaping across a river).

Try jumping on the spot from two feet. While you are in the air, find two ways to twist. While you are jumping, look over your shoulder at your feet.

"Wrestle" with your partner in slow motion. Do not actually touch each other, but try to show considerable force in your body movements so that we can see the effort you are using.

Decide what a hunter's actions are like and practice them with or without your partner.

Put a hunting sequence together. Include running, jumping, and wrestling.

SCORPION

Scorpion moves at lightning speed, crushing his victim and injecting a poison. The children will develop greater variety of movements if the teacher poses problems like the following:

Moving at lightning speed, see how far you can run before I bang the drum . . . Go! (The group will need to practice working for sudden movement with control.)

A scorpion crushes its prey with its front claws, afterward injecting poison into the victim with its tail. Make a very strong crushing action using your elbows (or one elbow and one knee, or two parts of your own choosing).

Another quite different movement will be required for injecting poison. Start from the position which is your scorpion shape. With part of your body make a stinging action. Use sharp, light movements and contrast them with strong, crushing actions. (Select one or two children for a demonstration.)

DEATHS

After Scorpion crushes Orion and injects the poison, Orion dies. Diana (invisible) then kills Scorpion. Both partners will, therefore, have to devise ways to suggest death. The teacher will help the children explore the movements with tasks like the following:

When a creature is suffering and dying, it writhes in pain, twisting and turning. Try to show that in your movement.

Gradually, as strength fails, the twisting and turning become weaker and weaker, slower and slower. Using the same movements, gradually slow your writhing and twisting.

Finish in your Scorpion or Orion shape.

Improvisation

Working in pairs, each child becomes either Orion or Scorpion. Those who are Orion develop a sequence that shows Orion experiencing "a hard day's hunt" and then lying down and falling asleep. Scorpion moves around the sleeping Orion and crushes him. Orion reacts with strong movements, only gradually weakening and dying. Scorpion then dies, struck down by an invisible goddess Diana. With lights off, a group of children arrange themselves around the floor in the pattern of the Orion constellation and shine their flashlights on the ceiling.

Accompaniments

Castanets-on-a-stick, making a series of short, sharp sounds can be excellent accompaniment for the scuttling actions of the scorpion. A combination of the hand drum and cymbals will be effective for Orion. Alternatively, music suggesting the cosmic may be used to create an intergalactic atmosphere. Some good choices might be Gustav Holst's *The Planets*, especially the part called "Venus, the Bringer of Peace" (Adrian Boult and the Birmingham Orchestra, Angel, S-36420) or Richard Strauss's *Also Sprach Zarathustra* (Eugene Ormandy and the Philadelphia Symphony, Columbia, M31829).

Extending the Lesson

Listed below are some outstanding children's books that will provide the class with background for further exploration of myths:

d'Aulaire, Ingri & Edgar. *Book of Greek Myths*. Garden City, N.Y.: Doubleday, 1962.

Evslin, Bernard; Evslin, Dorothy; & Hooppes, Ned. *Greek Gods*, New York, New York, Scholastic, 1966.

Farmer, Penelope. *Daedalus and Icarus*. New York: Harcourt Brace Jovanovich, 1971.

Garfield, Leon, & Blishen, Edward. *The God Beneath the Sea*. New York: Pantheon, 1973.

Garfield, Leon, & Blishen, Edward. *The Golden Shadow*. New York: Pantheon, 1973.

Gates, Doris. *The Golden God, Apollo*. New York: Viking, 1973.

Gates, Doris. *Lord of the Sky*. New York: Viking, Zeus, 1973.

Green, Roger Lancelyn. *A Book of Myths*. New York: Dutton, 1965.

Hodges, Margaret. *The Gorgon's Head*. Boston: Little, Brown, 1972.

Hodges, Margaret. *Persephone and the Springtime, A Greek Myth*. Boston: Little, Brown, 1973.

Serraillier, Ian. *The Clashing Rocks, the Story of Jason*. New York: Walck, 1964.

Serraillier, Ian. *A Fall From the Sky: The Story of Daedalus*. New York: Walck, 1966.

Serraillier, Ian. *The Gorgon's Head: The Story of Perseus*. New York: Walck, 1962.

Serraillier, Ian. *Heracles the Strong*. New York: Walck, 1970.

Serraillier, Ian. *The Way of Danger, The Story of Theseus*. New York: Walck, 1963.

White, Ann Terry. *The Golden Treasury of Myths and Legends*. New York: Golden Press, 1959.

When the children have read some of this material, the teacher should point out parallel stories and highlight differences and similarities between them. The group may then try writing their own modern myths. The children may also want to improvise their own dances around other myths.

LESSON 9: "PING PONG"

Every teacher who has ever had close contact with children knows that all through their years in school children play with language in innumerable ways, ranging from riddles to pig latin. In this lesson, young readers can explore the same fertile territory in a poem made up entirely of double words, the stimulus and accompaniment for a light-hearted game of ping pong in mime. The action for the mime must indicate the speed, direction, and level of the flight of the ball.

Ping Pong

Ping Pong
Wig Wag
Rick Rack
Zig Zag
Knick Knack
Gew Gaw
Riff Raff
See Saw

Criss Cross
Flip Flop
Ding Dong
Tip Top
Sing Song
Wish Wash
King Kong
  Bong.
      —Eve Merriam

Explorations

RHYTHM

After some discussion the two words of each pair are written on the blackboard (or on posters) in such a way that the children must turn their heads in order to read them. For example,

Wig . . . . Wag
Rick . . . . Rack
Zig . . . . Zag

This will give an immediate sense of a game in progress. The group next decides which part of the poem will be read very slowly and which quickly to speed "the game" up.

THROWS

The teacher can help the children achieve varied "throws" and "catches" with the following game:

All members of the class stand in a circle, fairly far apart. Each takes a turn throwing an imaginary ball which "changes" weight or size periodically as the teacher calls out a different ball—baseball, beach ball, basketball, tennis ball, ping pong ball, ball made of lead, etc. As the children throw, they call the name of the person who will "catch" the "ball." Throughout the game, all players follow "the ball" with their eyes.

ACCOMPANIMENT

The poem itself is the accompanying sound effect and must be practiced as if each word represented the bounce of a ball. Variation in speed and volume will give realism and interest to the sounds. Considerable concentration will be required in the mime to adjust to the imaginary flight of the ball and the timing of the accompaniment.

Improvisation

The class divides into groups of three: Two children "play" the game (ping pong) as the third reads the poem. Then they change places so that each has a turn playing and reading. It is up to the players to make their games realistic and interesting while leading up to some definite ending. They should place emphasis on:

- The strength of their hitting
- Watching their partners' stroke as well as their own
- Watching the imaginary flight of the ball
- Varying the direction, length, height of their shots
- Services and other breaks in the rally

The class can also "play" the game together. Two children are the players miming the game. Half the class sit on the sidelines watching an imaginary ball move back and forth between the players. The rest sit in a corner reciting the poem.

Extending the Lesson

The words in "Ping Pong" are all double words. The English language has many others. For example:

chin-chin	teeny-weeny	tick-tock
goody-goody	hokey-pokey	see-saw

Many games have been designed around double words. In one, Hink Pink, the players make up their own reduplicated combinations. For instance, someone poses a question that is to be answered with two or more rhyming words. Example:

Question: What makes people seasick?
Answer: Ocean motion.

Some sources for additional explorations in word play are:

Shipley, Joseph T. *Wordplay*. New York: Hawthorn, 1972.
Espy, Willard R. *The Game of Words*. New York: Grosset and
    Dunlap, 1971.

LESSON 10: THE THREE WITCHES

The remote, difficult language of poetry from another time can be made more accessible to children through movement. In this lesson, using scenes of the three witches in *Macbeth*, children gather and move around a "cauldron," exploring witch-like shapes and making "spells" as other children read the poem. This activity gives concrete meaning and great excitement to the poem's strange context and complicated incantations.

First Witch	:	When shall we three meet again,
		In thunder, lightning, or in rain?
Second Witch	:	When the hurlyburly's done,
		When the battle's lost and won.
Third Witch	:	That will be ere the set of sun.
First Witch	:	Where the place?
Second Witch	:	Upon the heath.

*   *   *

First Witch	:	Thrice the brinded cat hath mew'd.
Second Witch	:	Thrice; and once the hedge-pig whin'd.
Third Witch	:	Harper cries? — 'tis time, 'tis time.
First Witch	:	Round about the cauldron go;
		In the poison'd entrails throw.
		Toad, that under cold stone,
		Days and nights hast thirty-one
		Swelter'd venom sleeping got,
		Boil thou first i' the charmed pot.
All	:	Double, double toil and trouble;
		Fire, burn; and, cauldron, bubble.
Second Witch	:	Fillet of a fenny snake,
		In the cauldron boil and bake;
		Eye of newt, and toe of frog,

> Wool of bat, and tongue of dog,
> Adder's fork, and blind-worm's sting,
> Lizard's leg, and owlet's wing,
> For a charm of powerful trouble,
> Like a hell-broth boil and bubble.

All   : Double, double toil and trouble;
> Fire, burn; and, cauldron, bubble.

Third Witch : Scale of dragon; tooth of wolf;
> Witches' mummy; maw and gulf
> Of the ravin'd salt-sea shark;
> Root of hemlock, digg'd i' the dark; . . .
> Gall of goat; and slips of yew,
> Sliver'd in the moon's eclipse;
> Nose of Turk; and Tartar's lips; . . .
> Make the gruel thick and slab:
> Add thereto a tiger's chaudron,
> For the ingredients of our cauldron.

All   : Double, double toil and trouble;
> Fire, burn; and, cauldron, bubble.
>   —Shakespeare, *Macbeth*
>   I, ii, 1–7
>   IV, i, 1–36

Explorations

WITCH-LIKE SHAPES

The following suggestions will help children explore various possibilities:

Make your hands twisted and stiff. Do the same thing with your whole body.

Using the twisted, stiff shapes, make two witch-like shapes. Move from one to the other. Spin around on the spot. When the cymbals crash, freeze low to the ground.

To a drum accompaniment, move very stealthily and freeze in a high position, changing shape slowly.

MAKING "SPELLS"

Ask the children to try a variety of ideas like:

Make a "spell" by tracing a pattern or making a special sign in the air. Use lots of space.

Put "ingredients" into your cauldron from mid level, from high up.

Pounce on a moving object—from high, low.

ACCOMPANIMENT

Probably the class should first hear the poetry read by the teacher (or perhaps by an advanced drama student). A group of children may then plan a choral interpretation. (Probably the best way is for individuals to read the three witches' parts separately.) After practice, they perform the reading while the other children listen. During this exploration, and also later while the children improvise their movement sequences, the teacher can use drum and/or cymbals to emphasize rhythm or highlight the drama.

Improvisation

The children divide into groups of three. Each group stands around its own "cauldron"—a red highway cone or some other object large enough to hold a flashlight. With the room darkened, the children listen to the verse once more as they develop movement sequences around their "cauldrons." All groups move at the same time, "freezing" from time to time on a signal from the teacher. Each group repeatedly establishes a relationship in which two children are moving from a low position to a high one as the third moves into a stretched position. The group can change movement from slow to fast and then freeze.

Extending the Lesson

Read a simple version of *Macbeth* as follow-up; you will find an excellent one in *Enchanted Island: Stories from Shakespeare* (New York: Walck, 1964). More mature groups may enjoy the play itself.

BIBLIOGRAPHY: ADDITIONAL REFERENCES FOR THE INTERMEDIATE GRADES

Poems Suited to Improvisations

Browning, Robert. "Pippa's Song." In *Favorite Poems, Old and New,* edited by Helen Ferris. Garden City, N.Y.: Doubleday, 1957.

Cane, Melville. "Phosphorescence." In *The Reading of Poetry,* edited by William Sheldon, Nellie Lyons, and Polly Rouault. Boston: Allyn and Bacon, 1963.

Coatsworth, Elizabeth. "Swift Things are Beautiful." In *Time for Poetry,* edited by May Hill Arbuthnot and Shelton Root, Jr. Glenview, Ill.: Scott, Foresman, 1968.

Longfellow, Henry Wadsworth. "The Tide Rises; The Tide Falls." In *Poems to be Read Aloud to Children and by Children,* edited by Ann McGerran. New York: Nelson, 1965.

Miller, Mary Britton. "The Cat." In *Told Under the Silver Umbrella,* edited by Literature Committee, American Association for Childhood Education. New York: Macmillan, 1949.

Sandburg, Carl. "The Bee Song," from *Wind Song.* New York: Harcourt Brace Jovanovich, 1960.

Smith, William Jay. "Seal." In *Reflections on a Gift of a Watermelon Pickle,* edited by Stephen Dunning, Edward Lueders, and Hugh Smith. Glenview, Ill.: Scott, Foresman, 1966.

Sources on Developing Movement Around Language and Literature

Boorman, Joyce. *Creative Dance in Grades 4–6.* Don Mills, Ontario: Longmans, 1971.

Boorman, Joyce. *Dance and Language Experiences with Children.* Don Mills, Ontario: Longmans, 1973.

Bruce, Valerie. *Dance and Dance Drama in Education.* London: Pergamon Press, 1965.

North, Marion. *Movement Education.* New York: Dutton, 1973.

Sheehy, Emma. *Children Discover Music and Dance.* New York: Teachers College Press, 1968.

Afterword:
Sharing the Results

This book has emphasized links between the art of movement and the language arts. Because suggested plans for fostering this interplay were developed as regular school lessons, formal performances were not emphasized. Yet dance, like drama, belongs to the performing arts and surely poetry and stories are intended to be spoken as well as read. Quite naturally, teachers and children who have put considerable effort into choral reading, dance composition, lighting effects, and tape recording will have a strong urge to test their work before an audience.

Like so many things in life, school "performances" are a mixed blessing. Too often the selection process denies many children a potentially valuable experience, and the amount of time spent rehearsing becomes disproportionate and inappropriate for school life. Pressure on teacher and children is sometimes heavy, and adult values are often superimposed on the children's work to polish the final outcome. On the other hand, under the right conditions most children love to perform and make a great effort when they know they are going to have a live audience or perform before a video camera.

There are many workable and rewarding compromises between no exposure and overemphasis on performing before an audience. If we use the word "share" instead of "performance," several scenarios present themselves. In perhaps the least stressful situation, the children can share a finished work within the class itself. Through that experience, they will start learning to become sensitive and discriminating audiences, and, at the same time, they will learn to cope with speaking and moving before a group. If the dance compositions are of high quality, the principal, other teachers, or other classes can be invited to watch.

In another "sharing" option, the children's work can be recorded on videotape whenever equipment is available. This is an especially popular and valuable teaching device, which provides an ideal occasion for evaluation by the group together.

Finally, from time to time, parents—usually an indulgent audience—should be given the opportunity to watch their children's best work. If performing is treated as "sharing," the results can be highly satisfying. Like the father who asked, "When is the next one?" the parents who watch their children will see the event as an experience in which they and their children can take pride.

Teachers who lack background in movement and dance need not feel hesitant about this extension of the language arts. The most important skill for them to learn is observing, a skill that can be acquired quickly. Mikhael Mordkin, Russian ballet dance master, put it very well when he said, "Dancing is not an art of the feet. It is an act of the imagination, of the head, and the heart." This book links the arts of language and movement so that the head and the heart are engaged and the imagination is stimulated.

Index